Sanjeev Kapoor's

NO-OIL Cooking

In association with Alyona Kapoor

Popular Prakashan
www.popularprakashan.com

Published by
POPULAR PRAKASHAN PVT. LTD.
301, Mahalaxmi Chambers
22, Bhulabhai Desai Road
Mumbai - 400026
for KHANA KHAZANA PUBLICATIONS PVT. LTD.

First Published 2006
Fourth Reprint July 2011 (Paperback Edition)

ISBN 978-81-7991-665-0
(4413)

Book Design	:	Creative Quotient (CQ-A Repro India LimitedEnterprise)
Photography	:	Mangesh Parab
Food Stylist	:	Harpal Singh Sokhi
Nutritionists	:	Prachi Hatwalne & Kirti Masurkar

Printed in India
by Nutech Photolithographers
B-240, Okhla Ind. Area, Phase - I
New Delhi - 110020

Author's Note

Life is more fun and interesting if there is a challenge before you. This book was definitely interesting to write and of course challenging because my focus was totally on making oil-free food look great and taste good. And believe me, gone are the morose days when oil-free meant boiled steamed food with a dash of salt and pepper. It does not mean *khichdi* and *dahi* any more. Mealtimes are eminently more fulfilling if there is some access to recipes that you can enjoy along with the family given the fact that the food has to be oil-free.

A lot has been said and written about "low oil" or "no oil" diets, but how well the subject has been understood is the moot question. Modern life brings with it loads of stress, tension and related health problems. The progress in science has introduced various gadgets and means to relieve physical strain but then that very relief has given rise to ailments : though we have adjusted to the modern way of life we have not really been able to adjust our diet accordingly. The idea for this book took seed from here and you would be interested to know about the making of this book. I should say let us forget the journey but enjoy the final destination: in other words, my recipes are for everyday cooking. In this day and age when middle age diseases referred to so nonchalantly as 'lifestyle diseases' are on the rise, I am sure some of you would welcome this new addition to the kitchen. There are recipes for all courses in a meal, and each of them has been totally researched and perfected.

Oil has always been an important constituent of most cuisines around the world for it not only adds taste, but also imparts its own flavour. For example, coconut oil, olive oil, mustard oil etc. But along with the flavours comes the high fat content and the dense calories which are restricted for some of us for medical reasons. As you go along the book you will see that we have tried not to use any oil or ghee or cream or even certain ingredients with a high fat content. But at the same time, great care has been taken to ensure that the taste factor has not been much affected.

These recipes are meant not only for weight-watchers, they are for you and me who are health conscious, who want to look better, live better and longer! My mantra is to eat well but sensibly and follow a regular exercise regime. These recipes are suggestions to bring a change into the daily diet and by all means, use them whenever the need is to try out oil-free cooking.

Each active person is allowed 15 grams of visible fat a day. But the truth is that we end up having a lot more than the allowed quantity because most of us are unaware that all foods contain some percentage of fat. Be it wheat, pulses, vegetables, fruits, skimmed milk, cottage cheese, yogurt, cloves, cinnamon, sesame seeds and even the miniscule single mustard seed! So if we do eat a variety of foods each day, in a variety of menus, balancing the carbohydrate and protein intake, all invisible fat included in this way is just perfect for a healthy diet. My point here is that "no oil" does not mean that the food is totally free of lipid content.

It is important to keep the taste buds pampered because they rule the roost! The contents of this book do just that. All the recipes are written to provide for four portions. The portion size has been set keeping in mind that they form part of a menu which will have other complementary dishes and will be shared by a group of people.

So just tie up your aprons and armed with non-stick cookware try out this wonderful array of dishes that will not only help you live a healthy life but will also win hearts along the way.

Happy Cooking!

From Our Nutritionists' Desk

The purpose of giving you these oil free recipes is to bring some newness to your daily diet. We live in a world that is moving at breakneck speed. And in this stressed style of living, more and more people face the problem of raised cholesterol levels. And if this is not scary enough, we have life style diseases like obesity, diabetes and hypertension. Hence the pressing needs to decrease the intake of oil and fats.

The Need of the Hour

It would be perfectly correct to say that high cholesterol levels are also a result of a lack of exercise and regard for good health. Lack of time causes neglect of things that matter: like looking after one own's self, following a healthy eating pattern and also incorporating an exercise schedule into one's daily routine. Now is the time to tighten our belts simply because more and more young people seem to be suffering from all sorts of life style diseases that shorten life spans. This book presents a gentle guideline for eating low fat food, which is made without the addition of seed extracted oil.

Learn to Switch

Many people wonder about the pros and cons of an oil free diet. The important fact to remember is that we cannot do without oil. But we can certainly do with less oil in our food. And the sooner we adopt a fat free mode of cooking the better for our health in the long run. One weak moment of hunger that made you demolish a samosa adds a whopping 369 calories to your day's intake. Or have a small 105 grams pack of your favourite French fries, which will add 360 calories. Instead, two idlis will provide only 60 calories and be just as filling. Small things make a difference: switching over from buffalo's milk to cow's milk saves up to 50 calories and 2.4 grams of fat per 100 grams. The time has come to make your choices.

It is not really an Oil-Free World

You will realize while browsing through the book that we have not used any visible oil in the recipes. One can easily be led to think that an oil-free world exists. But it does not. The fact is, all foods contain some trace of oil fat like poppy seeds, coriander seeds, cumin seeds, cloves, peppercorns, sesame seeds and turmeric powder do have some fat content. These ingredients have been used in almost all the recipes ensuring that they are not misjudged as being 'fat free'. They are `low fat' and there are no great health hazards in having low fat foods. For those who are concerned it would be interesting to know that a hundred grams of poppy seeds contain 19.3 grams of fat. Similarly, cashew nuts, groundnuts, dried coconut, fresh coconut, almonds and walnuts also have considerable amounts of fat. Well, even arhar/toovar dal has a fat content - 100 grams has 1.5 grams of fat as compared to 3.7 in a moong dal preparation. Dals are not eaten raw and once they are cooked they do have additions of seeds and spices.

We Do Need Oil

Our bodily functions operate at the optimum when they are lubricated well and for all this all naturally present oils are good. We are all aware that oil adds taste and an appetizing appearance to anything you make. Yes, even some salads taste better with a dash of salad oil or olive oil. Oil is an integral part of most recipes because it removes the unpalatability of the dish and adds the needed softness, flavour and nutrients.

Some reasons why we need fat:

- Fat is a concentrated source of energy and is essential for the absorption of fat soluble vitamins.
- It is an important constituent of cells and helps in growth and development.
- Fat consists of Essential Fatty Acids (EFA). A no-fat diet deprives the body of these EFA and it could lead to growth retardation, skin lesions and liver degeneration. Dryness and scaliness of skin have also been observed.
- EFA are so named because they cannot be processed or manufactured by the body. They play an important role in growth, reproduction, skin and hair conditions and healing of wounds. They also play a structural role in cell membranes.

Weight loss and no-fat go together. But a long term no-fat diet is undesirable as it can lead to some serious problems like :

- Dry, itchy and scaling skin
- Dry, dull and and dandruff-ridden hair
- Poor healing of wounds
- Neurological disease
- Heart disease (arteriosclerosis)
- Skin diseases
- Degenerative conditions such as cataract, arthritis and cancer.

It is better to follow a diet that is low in fat but healthy in essential proteins, carbohydrates, vitamins and minerals. A good diet is primarily what we should be looking at. Hence this book of recipes that have been made without oil. If you have binged one day, the following day or two try making use of the recipes in this book.

And remember...
Eat sensibly, exercise and have a long and healthy life!

Contents

Main Course - Seafood, Chicken and Mutton

Accompaniments

Sweets

Annexure

Moroccan Mint Tea

INGREDIENTS

2 teaspoons tea leaves

16 fresh mint leaves

4 lemons, cut into wedges

2 inches cinnamon

4 star anise (*chakri phool*)

16 teaspoons caster sugar

1 Place tea leaves, mint leaves, lemon wedges, cinnamon, star anise and caster sugar in a teapot.

2 Pour boiling water, cover the teapot and allow to infuse for about three to four minutes. Stir well to dissolve the sugar. Pour into individual glasses and serve hot.

Veg | Preparation 6 mins | Cooking 5 mins | Serves 4 people

Kiwi *ka Panna*

INGREDIENTS

4 kiwi fruit

¼ cup fresh mint leaves, chopped

¼ cup fresh coriander leaves, chopped

½ teaspoon cumin seeds, roasted

½ inch piece ginger, chopped

5-6 black peppercorns

3 tablespoons sugar

Salt to taste

1 teaspoon black salt

1 tablespoon lemon juice

Crushed ice, as required

1 Roast kiwi fruit in a *tandoor* or in an oven at 150°C/300°F/Gas Mark 2 for half an hour or till soft. Cool, peel and crush in a bowl with your fingers or with a wooden spoon, to a smooth pulp. Grind mint leaves, coriander leaves, cumin seeds, ginger and peppercorns to a smooth paste.

2 Blend kiwi pulp with sugar, salt, black salt and lemon juice. Add mint-coriander paste and mix well. Strain. Add four cups of water and stir well to mix. Put some ice cubes into individual glasses, pour the *panna* over and serve chilled.

Veg | Preparation 30 mins | Cooking 10 mins | Serves 4 people

Moroccan *Mint Tea*

Kiwi *ka Panna*

INGREDIENTS

5 medium bananas, roughly chopped

5 tablespoons honey

2 tablespoons lemon juice

2 cups drained skimmed milk yogurt

10 ice cubes

10 fresh mint leaves, torn

Banana *and Honey Smoothie*

1 Place roughly chopped bananas in a freezer for one hour. Place the frozen banana pieces, honey, lemon juice and yogurt in a blender and blend until smooth.

2 Add ice cubes and blend again. Pour into individual glasses and serve garnished with mint leaves.

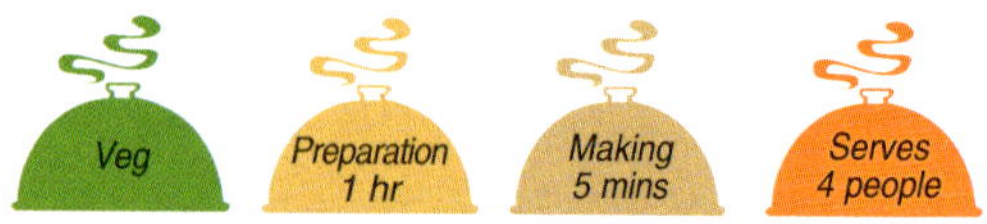

INGREDIENTS

½ small musk melon, cut into ½ inch cubes

6 oranges

½ medium watermelon, seeded and roughly chopped

½ teaspoon *chaat masala*

Musk Melon *in Orange Juice*

1 Squeeze out juice of oranges. Strain and set aside. Blend watermelon pieces in a blender till smooth. Strain.

2 Mix orange juice and watermelon juice. Add *chaat masala* and mix well. Chill.

3 To serve, put one-fourth of the musk melon cubes in each serving glass and pour the blended juice over.

4 Serve immediately.

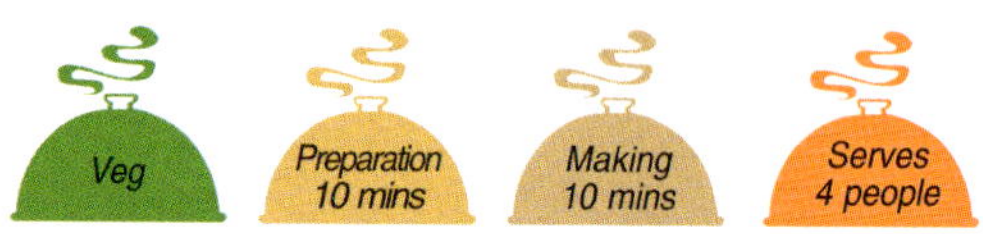

Sweetcorn *and* Prawn *Chowder*

INGREDIENTS

½ cup sweetcorn, cream style
16-20 small prawns, peeled and deveined
4 medium potatoes, quartered
1 medium onion, quartered
2 inches celery stalk, roughly broken
Salt to taste
1 small green capsicum, seeded and cut into small pieces
8-10 black peppercorns, crushed

FOR THE PRAWN STOCK

10-12 prawn heads and shells
1 bay leaf
5-6 black peppercorns
2 inches celery stalk, roughly broken
1 medium onion, quartered
½ medium carrot, sliced

1 To make prawn stock, clean, wash and roast prawn heads under a preheated grill for eight to ten minutes. Place in a thick-bottomed pan along with shells, bay leaf, peppercorns, celery, onion and carrot. Add five cups of water and bring to a boil. Reduce heat, cover and simmer for eight to ten minutes. Strain the stock through a piece of muslin and set aside.

2 Cook the potatoes, onion, celery, half of the sweetcorn along with two cups of prawn stock and salt in a thick-bottomed pan till soft. Strain and reserve the liquid. Cool, process the potato mixture in a blender, adding the reserved liquid as required, till smooth.

3 Transfer the blended potato mixture back into the pan, add the remaining stock, capsicum and remaining sweetcorn. Cover and cook on low heat for two minutes. Add prawns and continue to cook for another two minutes.

4 Add crushed peppercorns, adjust seasoning and consistency and cook for a minute. Pour into individual soup bowls and serve hot, with breadsticks.

Sweetcorn *and* Prawn *Chowder*

Tomato *and* Basil *Soup*

Tomato

and Basil Soup

INGREDIENTS

20-24 medium tomatoes, quartered

24 fresh basil leaves

2 bay leaves

20 black peppercorns

2 medium onions, sliced

8 garlic cloves, chopped

2 six-inch celery stalks, finely chopped

2 medium carrots, roughly chopped

Salt to taste

2 tablespoons gram flour (*besan*)

2 teaspoons sugar

1 Heat a non-stick pan. Add bay leaves, half the peppercorns and onions and roast until the onions turn translucent.

2 Add garlic, celery and three tablespoons of water. Stir and add carrots and tomatoes.

3 Reserve six basil leaves for garnishing and add the rest to the tomatoes. Stir and add salt.

4 Cook on medium heat till the tomatoes soften. Add three cups of water and bring to a boil. Cover and cook for ten to fifteen minutes.

5 Pass mixture through a strainer and reserve the liquid. Remove peppercorns and bay leaves from the residue and allow it to cool. Process in a blender to get a smooth purée.

6 Roast gram flour in another pan till fragrant. Add the puréed tomatoes and mix. Add reserved liquid and adjust consistency.

7 Place the pan on heat. Add sugar, salt, remaining peppercorns, freshly crushed, and let the soup simmer for a couple of minutes. Strain and bring to a boil again.

8 Garnish with the reserved basil leaves and serve piping hot.

Veg | Preparation 15 mins | Cooking 25 mins | Serves 4 people

Kale Gajar *ki Kanji*

INGREDIENTS

4 large black carrots (*kali gajar*)

4 tablespoons mustard seeds, coarsely powdered

3 tablespoons salt

1½ tablespoons coarse red chilli powder

Chef's Tip: *If black carrots are not available, try the same kanji with red carrots. But try you must!*

1 Scrub carrots and wash under running water. Peel and cut carrots into batons. Take eighteen cups of water in a large jar or a clay pot (*matka*), which will be able to hold four litres of water. Add carrots, mustard powder, salt and red chilli powder and mix well.

2 Cover the pot with a piece of muslin and tie it around the rim. Let it stand in the sun for three to four days. Refrigerate when ready. Stir well before serving. Pour into tall glasses with pieces of carrot. Serve chilled.

Veg | Preparation 10 mins | Maturing 3-4 days | Serves 4 people

Belfal *Sherbet*

INGREDIENTS

1 stone apple (*belfal/siriphal*)

1 cup sugar

Crushed ice, as required

1 Break open the shell of the fruit. Remove seeds and scoop out flesh with the help of a spoon. Soak the flesh in water for a few hours. Strain the pulp through a sieve.Place sugar with three cups of water in a pan. Heat till sugar dissolves.

2 Strain sugar syrup through a piece of muslin. Cool completely. Place fruit pulp and sugar syrup in a blender. Blend till smooth. Strain through a sieve. Serve chilled in tall glasses with lots of crushed ice.

Veg | Preparation 2 hrs | Cooking 20 mins | Serves 4 people

Red Capsicum

Soup with Lemon

INGREDIENTS

8 medium red capsicums

4 tablespoons lemon juice

2 medium onions, chopped

12 garlic cloves, chopped

1 tablespoon refined flour (*maida*)

5 cups Vegetable Stock (pg. 120)

4-5 fresh basil leaves

Salt to taste

1 teaspoon sugar

5-6 black peppercorns, crushed

1 Prick red capsicums with a fork, and roast them directly on a low flame till lightly charred. Plunge into cold water, remove skin and chop roughly.

2 Put onions and garlic into a non-stick pan and roast on medium heat for a minute. Add refined flour and continue to roast for another minute till lightly browned or till it emits a pleasant aroma.

3 Add one cup of vegetable stock, the capsicums and a couple of fresh basil leaves. Stir and bring to a boil. Cover and simmer for three to four minutes. Cool and blend to a smooth purée.

4 Transfer into a thick-bottomed pan, add the remaining stock and bring to a boil.

5 Reduce heat, add salt, sugar and crushed peppercorns. Simmer for two to three minutes.

6 Add lemon juice, stir and pour into individual soup bowls. Serve hot, garnished with remaining fresh basil leaves.

Red Capsicum

Soup with Lemon

Apple, Pineapple and Orange

Salad

INGREDIENTS

1 large apple, diced

½ medium fresh pineapple, diced

2 medium oranges, segmented

10 fresh mint leaves

FOR THE DRESSING

1 tablespoon lemon juice

1 teaspoon sugar

Salt to taste

½ teaspoon roasted cumin seeds, crushed

½ teaspoon red chilli flakes

5-6 black peppercorns, crushed

Apple, *Pineapple* and Orange *Salad*

1. Mix together all the ingredients for the dressing along with two tablespoons of water.
2. Mix together prepared apple, pineapple and orange. Add the dressing and toss well to mix.
3. Serve garnished with roughly torn mint leaves.

Veg | Preparation 10 mins | Making 5 mins | Serves 4 people

Hot and Sour Chicken Soup

INGREDIENTS

¼ cup chicken, boiled and chopped
1 slice bamboo shoot
3 tablespoons cornflour
1 small onion, chopped
2-3 garlic cloves, chopped
1 inch ginger, grated
2 inches celery stalk, chopped
½ medium carrot, grated
1 small piece cabbage, chopped
2 fresh button mushrooms, chopped
½ medium green capsicum, seeded and chopped
2 French beans, chopped
½ teaspoon white pepper powder
Salt to taste
½ teaspoon sugar
½ teaspoon MSG (optional)
2 tablespoons soy sauce
2 tablespoons green chilli sauce
4-5 cups Chicken Stock (pg. 120)
2 tablespoons vinegar
1 stalk spring onion greens, chopped

1 Boil the bamboo shoot in one cup of water for two to three minutes, drain, cool and chop finely.

2 Mix cornflour and half a cup of water.

3 Heat a non-stick wok or a saucepan, add onion, garlic, ginger and cook for a few seconds. Add celery, carrot, cabbage, bamboo shoot, mushroom, capsicum and French beans.

4 Cook for two to three minutes or until vegetables are almost cooked, stirring continuously. Add chicken and cook for one minute more.

5 Add white pepper powder, salt to taste, sugar, MSG, soy sauce, green chilli sauce and mix well.

6 Stir in chicken stock and bring to a boil. Stir in cornflour mixture and continue to cook for a minute or until the soup thickens.

7 Stir in vinegar and serve piping hot, garnished with spring onion greens.

Chef's tip: *We have used tinned bamboo shoot slices, which are preserved in brine, hence they should be boiled in water for two to three minutes before use.*

Non-Veg | Preparation 20 mins | Cooking 10 mins | Serves 4 people

Clear *Vegetable Soup*

INGREDIENTS

6-8 fresh button mushrooms, sliced

½ medium carrot, thinly sliced

4-6 leaves Chinese cabbage, cut into 1 inch pieces

1 inch celery stalk, diagonally sliced

1 spring onion, sliced

1 medium red capsicum, seeded, cut into 1 inch pieces

8-10 snow peas, halved

12-16 spinach leaves, chopped

4-5 cups Vegetable Stock (pg. 120)

2-3 garlic cloves, crushed

¼ teaspoon MSG (optional)

3-4 black peppercorns, crushed

Salt to taste

½ cup bean sprouts

½ teaspoon lemon juice (optional)

1 Heat vegetable stock in a wok or a pan, add crushed garlic and bring to a boil. Add mushrooms, carrot, Chinese cabbage, celery, spring onion, red capsicum, snow peas and spinach and cook for two to three minutes after it starts boiling again.

2 Add MSG, crushed peppercorns, salt and bean sprouts. Stir in lemon juice and serve piping hot.

Veg | Preparation 15 mins | Cooking 10 mins | Serves 4 people

Coriander Prawn and Mango Salad

INGREDIENTS

¾ cup small prawns, peeled and deveined

½ cup Green Coriander Chutney (pg. 32)

1 small green unripe mango, peeled and cut into fine strips

2 medium tomatoes

1 teaspoon mustard paste

Salt to taste

4-5 tablespoons sugar

7-8 black peppercorns, crushed

1 teaspoon lemon juice

4-5 leaves iceberg lettuce, chilled in iced water

1. Halve the tomatoes, remove the seeds and cut into strips.
2. Marinate prawns in green coriander chutney for about fifteen minutes.
3. Heat a *tawa* and cook prawns till they are done.
4. Mix together mango, tomato, mustard paste, salt, sugar, crushed peppercorns, lemon juice and one tablespoon of water.
5. Add the cooked prawns and toss to mix.
6. Serve on a bed of chilled, crisp lettuce.

Non-Veg | Preparation 10 mins | Cooking 10 mins | Serves 4 people

Coriander Prawn *and* Mango *Salad*

INGREDIENTS

30 spinach leaves, finely chopped

3 medium potatoes, boiled and mashed

1 medium onion, finely chopped

4 cups Vegetable Stock (pg. 120)

Salt to taste

½ teaspoon black pepper powder

½ cup skimmed milk

Caldo Verde

-Spinach and

Potato Soup

1 Heat a deep non-stick pan. Add onion and cook for a couple of minutes taking care that the colour of the onion does not change.

2 Add vegetable stock and bring to a boil.

3 Add mashed potatoes and stir well to mix. Add spinach and cook till the leaves soften. Add salt to taste and black pepper powder.

4 Stir in the milk and bring to a boil and cook for a minute or two more.

5 Serve piping hot.

Veg | Preparation 15 mins | Cooking 15 mins | Serves 4 people

Garlic-flavoured Rasam

INGREDIENTS

15-20 garlic cloves

2 tablespoons split pigeon peas (*toovar/arhar dal*), soaked

1 medium tomato, chopped

2 teaspoons tamarind pulp

Salt to taste

A pinch of asafoetida

¼ teaspoon turmeric powder

FOR THE RASAM POWDER

1 teaspoon cumin seeds

6-8 black peppercorns

4 whole red chillies

1 tablespoon coriander seeds

1 teaspoon split Bengal gram (*chana dal*)

FOR TEMPERING

½ teaspoon mustard seeds

2 whole red chillies

1 sprig curry leaves

1. Heat a non-stick pan. Roast garlic cloves for a minute. Remove and set aside.

2. Boil three cups of water in a deep pan. Add *dal* and tomato and cook, covered, till soft. Mash and reserve along with the water.

3. Make the *rasam* powder : In a non-stick pan dry roast cumin seeds, peppercorns, whole red chillies, coriander seeds and split Bengal gram to a light brown colour. Cool and pound to a fine powder.

4. Add three more cups of water to the tamarind pulp and boil with salt, asafoetida, turmeric powder and the *rasam* powder for five minutes or till the raw smell of the tamarind disappears.

5. Add mashed *dal* to the *rasam* and bring to a boil. Reduce heat and simmer for five minutes. Strain and bring to a boil again.

6. For tempering, dry roast mustard seeds, red chillies and curry leaves in a non-stick pan and add to the strained *rasam*. Cover immediately to trap the flavours and serve piping hot, garnished with roasted garlic.

Chef's Tip: *You can pound the garlic very lightly before adding to give a better and stronger flavour. Increase or decrease the garlic to suit your taste.*

Veg | Preparation 10 mins | Cooking 30 mins | Serves 4 people

Seafood Soup

INGREDIENTS

1 small black pomfret, skinned and filleted

1 small squid

16 small prawns, peeled and deveined

5 cups fish stock

1 lemon grass stalk, sliced diagonally

1 inch celery stalk, chopped

1 inch ginger, grated

4 medium fresh button mushrooms, thinly sliced

Salt to taste

¼ teaspoon black pepper powder

2 fresh red chillies, thinly sliced

2 stalks spring onion greens, sliced

½ teaspoon lemon juice

1. Cut fish fillets into half inch cubes and set aside. Clean, wash and cut the squid into rings.
2. Blanch prawns, fish and squid in three to four cups of boiling salted water for a minute. Drain, refresh in cold water and set aside.
3. Heat fish stock in a wok and bring to a boil. Reduce heat, add lemon grass, celery, ginger, button mushrooms, salt and pepper powder and simmer for two to three minutes.
4. Add the blanched prawns, fish and squid along with fresh red chillies; cover and simmer for another two minutes.
5. Add spring onion greens and lemon juice. Adjust seasoning, stir and simmer for one more minute.
6. Pour into soup bowls and serve hot.

Note: *To make fish stock, boil together 200 grams of fish bones, head, skin (any unutilised portion of fish), five cups of water, 1 medium sliced onion, 1 sliced mushroom, 3 inch stalk of celery, chopped, 1 bay leaf and 4-6 peppercorns in a pan. Remove scum and simmer for fifteen minutes. Strain and use.*

Non-Veg | Preparation 15 mins | Cooking 10 mins | Serves 4 people

INGREDIENTS

1 slice brown bread, toasted, cut into 1 inch pieces

2 medium onions

1 medium green capsicum, seeded, cut into 1 inch pieces

2 medium tomatoes, seeded, cut into 1 inch pieces

1 small head iceberg lettuce, torn into bite-size pieces

2 tablespoons brown breadcrumbs, toasted

FOR THE DRESSING

2 tablespoons vinegar

Salt to taste

7-8 black peppercorns, crushed

6 small pickled gherkins, chopped

1 teaspoon dried rosemary

¼ teaspoon mixed herbs

Bread Salad

with Roasted Onions

1 Roast onions over an open flame. Cut into one inch square pieces.

2 For the dressing mix together vinegar, salt, crushed peppercorns, pickled gherkins, rosemary and mixed herbs.

3 Mix together bread cubes, onions, capsicum, tomato and iceberg lettuce in a bowl.

4 Just before serving, add the dressing and toss to mix. Garnish with toasted brown breadcrumbs and serve immediately.

Veg | Preparation 10 mins | Cooking 5 mins | Serves 4 people

INGREDIENTS

200 grams boneless chicken, boiled and shredded

1 cup farfalle (bow-tie pasta)

1 medium tomato, cut into ½ inch cubes

1 medium carrot, cut into ½ inch cubes

½ medium green capsicum, seeded, cut into ½ inch cubes

½ medium yellow capsicum, seeded, cut into ½ inch cubes (optional)

8-10 olives, cut into rings

FOR THE DRESSING

4-5 garlic cloves, chopped

2 inches celery stalk, finely chopped

½ teaspoon crushed red chillies

2-3 tablespoons lemon juice

Salt to taste

2 teaspoons finely chopped fresh parsley

Tropical Chicken *and Farfalle Salad*

1 Boil three cups of water in a deep pan. Add pasta and cook till just done. Drain and set aside to cool.

2 To make the dressing combine garlic, celery, red chillies, lemon juice, salt and parsley. Mix well.

3 In a bowl mix together pasta, chicken, tomato, carrot, green capsicum, yellow capsicum and olives. Pour the prepared dressing over and toss to mix. Serve immediately.

Non-Veg | Preparation 20 mins | Cooking 10 mins | Serves 4 people

Tropical Chicken *and* Farfalle *Salad*

Vegetable Ribbon Salad

INGREDIENTS

- 1 medium zucchini, peeled
- 2 medium carrots, peeled
- 2 medium cucumbers, peeled
- Salt to taste
- 5 black olives, sliced

FOR THE DRESSING

- 2 tablespoons vinegar
- 1 tablespoon soy sauce
- 1 teaspoon brown sugar
- ¼ teaspoon red chilli flakes
- 3-4 fresh basil leaves

1. Take a potato peeler or a manual slicer and slice zucchini, carrots and cucumbers lengthways into thin ribbons. Sprinkle a little salt and set aside for five minutes.
2. Blend vinegar, soy sauce, brown sugar, red chilli flakes, roughly torn basil leaves and salt to make a coarse paste. Transfer to a bowl.
3. Squeeze the cut vegetables to remove excess liquid. Add vegetables to the dressing in the bowl and toss well. Serve garnished with olive slices.

Veg | Preparation 10 mins | Making 5 mins | Serves 4 people

Mushrooms in Balsamic Vinegar

INGREDIENTS

- 400 grams fresh button mushrooms, quartered
- Salt to taste
- 2 teaspoons garlic paste
- 5-6 fresh basil leaves
- 5 tablespoons sugar
- 2 teaspoons balsamic vinegar
- 7-8 black peppercorns, crushed

1. Marinate mushrooms in a mixture of salt, garlic paste and roughly torn basil leaves for two hours. Heat sugar in a pan. Add one tablespoon of water, stir continuously till it caramelises to a light golden colour.
2. Add balsamic vinegar and crushed peppercorns and cook for three to four minutes. Toss mushrooms in caramelised sugar mixture and refrigerate. Serve chilled.

Veg | Preparation 2 hrs | Cooking 10 mins | Serves 4 people

Warm Potato Salad

with Green Beans

INGREDIENTS

8-10 baby potatoes

10-12 French beans, cut into 1 inch pieces

½ teaspoon paprika or crushed red chilli

FOR THE DRESSING

2 tablespoons *paneer* (made from skimmed milk), crumbled

½ cup skimmed milk yogurt

1 teaspoon mustard paste

Salt to taste

7-8 black peppercorns, crushed

2 stalks spring onion greens, chopped

1. Boil potatoes in two cups of water, drain and set aside. Boil French beans in one cup of water, drain and refresh in cold water. Set aside.
2. Mix together baby potatoes leaving the skin on, and French beans and set aside.
3. For the dressing, mix *paneer*, yogurt, mustard paste, salt, crushed peppercorns and spring onion greens.
4. Fold the baby potatoes and French beans into the prepared dressing. Adjust seasoning.
5. Sprinkle paprika or crushed red chilli on top and serve.

Veg

Preparation 15 mins

Cooking 10 mins

Serves 4 people

INGREDIENTS

2 large potatoes, boiled, peeled and cut into 1 inch cubes

1 large sweet potato, boiled, peeled and cut into 1 inch cubes

1½ tablespoons lemon juice

Salt to taste

1 inch ginger, cut into fine strips

1 large ripe banana

2 tablespoons tamarind pulp

2 green chillies, finely chopped

1 teaspoon *chaat masala*

2 tablespoons fresh coriander leaves, finely chopped

Aloo Kachalu

Chaat

1 Add half a teaspoon of lemon juice and a pinch of salt to ginger strips. Refrigerate.

2 Peel and cut banana into one inch pieces, mix with half a teaspoon of lemon juice and set aside.

3 Place potatoes, sweet potato and banana in a mixing bowl. Add remaining lemon juice, tamarind pulp, green chillies, *chaat masala*, salt to taste and coriander leaves; toss lightly.

4 Serve garnished with chilled pickled ginger strips.

Veg

Preparation 15 mins

Making 5 mins

Serves 4 people

Aloo Kachalu

Chaat

Sandwich Dhokla

INGREDIENTS

1 cup rice

¼ cup split black gram (*dhuli urad dal*)

¼ cup sour skimmed milk yogurt

Salt to taste

2 teaspoons ginger paste

1½ teaspoons green chilli paste

½ teaspoon soda bicarbonate

1 tablespoon lemon juice

½ cup thick Green Coriander Chutney (see below)

2 tablespoons fresh coriander leaves, chopped

1 Dry roast rice and *dal* on a *tawa* on medium heat for four to five minutes. Cool and grind to a slightly coarse powder. Put the rice powder into a bowl. Add yogurt and one and a half cups of warm water. Mix thoroughly to make a smooth batter of pouring consistency. Add salt, cover and let the batter ferment for eight to ten hours.

2 Once the batter has fermented, add ginger paste and green chilli paste and mix well. Boil water as required in a *dhokla* steamer. Pour half the batter into another bowl. In a small bowl mix one-fourth teaspoon of soda bicarbonate and half a tablespoon of lemon juice. Add this to half the batter and whisk well.

3 Repeat this procedure with the remaining batter just before putting it into the steamer. Pour the batter with the soda bicarbonate into a *thali* and place it in the steamer. Steam for eight to ten minutes. Check for doneness with a knife. If the knife comes out clean, it is cooked.

4 Remove from the steamer and spread green coriander chutney over the surface while the *dhokla* is hot. Pour remaining batter over the chutney and steam again for ten minutes. Remove from steamer, cool slightly, and garnish with coriander leaves. Cut into desired shapes and serve hot.

Note: *To make* ***Green Coriander Chutney****, grind together 1 cup fresh coriander leaves, ½ cup fresh mint leaves, 2-3 green chillies, black salt to taste, ¼ teaspoon sugar and 1 tablespoon lemon juice to a smooth paste using a little water if required.*

Veg | *Preparation 8-10 hrs* | *Cooking 20 mins* | *Serves 4 people*

INGREDIENTS

½ cup rice flour, sifted

8 tablespoons skimmed milk yogurt, whisked

Salt to taste

1 teaspoon green chilli paste

½ teaspoon ginger paste

½ teaspoon soda bicarbonate

8 banana leaves, cut into 5 inch squares or circles

FOR THE STUFFING

½ cup sprouted green gram (*ankurit moong*)

Salt to taste

3-4 black peppercorns, crushed

¼ teaspoon red chilli flakes

Rice

Panki

1 Put the rice flour into a bowl. Add yogurt and salt and mix well. Add green chilli paste and ginger paste and mix again. Add enough water to make a batter of pouring consistency. Add soda bicarbonate and mix. Cover and set aside to ferment for about two hours.

2 Mix all the ingredients for the stuffing together.

3 Heat a non-stick *tawa*.

4 Pour rice batter on each banana leaf, place the stuffing in the centre and fold the leaf into half. Place it on the *tawa* and cook for two to three minutes. Turn and cook the other side as well.

5 Serve the *panki* in the banana leaf.

Caribbean Chicken *Kebabs*

INGREDIENTS

4 (200 grams each) boneless chicken breasts, cut into 1 inch pieces

5-6 whole dried red chillies, seeded

2 medium onions

8-10 garlic cloves

2-3 fresh parsley sprigs

7-8 fresh basil leaves

½ tablespoon lemon juice

1 tablespoon Worcestershire sauce

5-6 black peppercorns

½ teaspoon curry powder

Salt to taste

1 medium green capsicum, seeded, cut into 1 inch pieces

2 slices canned pineapple, cut into 1 inch pieces

1 medium tomato, seeded, cut into 1 inch pieces

1. Chop one onion and cut the other into one inch square pieces.
2. Make a coarse paste of whole red chillies, chopped onion, garlic, parsley, basil, lemon juice, Worcestershire sauce, peppercorns, curry powder and salt. Transfer the paste into a bowl and add the chicken pieces. Mix well.
3. Add capsicum, pineapple, tomato and onion and marinate for two hours preferably in a refrigerator.
4. Thread chicken, capsicum, pineapple, tomato and onion pieces one after the other onto skewers. Reserve the remaining marinade for basting.
5. Heat a non-stick *tawa*. Place the skewers on the *tawa* and cook, basting with the reserved marinade half way through, for ten to twelve minutes or until chicken is done, rotating the skewers continuously.
6. Serve hot.

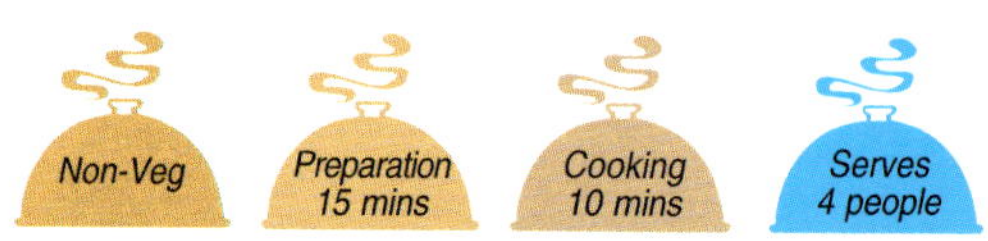

INGREDIENTS

FOR THE CHEELA

2 cups gram flour (*besan*)

¼ teaspoon soda bicarbonate

Salt to taste

1 teaspoon red chilli powder

1 teaspoon carom seeds (*ajwain*)

A pinch of asafoetida

2 tablespoons fresh coriander leaves, chopped

FOR THE STUFFING

2 medium onions, chopped

1 cup fresh fenugreek leaves (*methi*), chopped

8-10 fresh button mushrooms, sliced

2½ cups skimmed milk cottage cheese (*paneer*), grated

Salt to taste

¼ teaspoon black pepper powder

Stuffed Methi Cheela

1 For the stuffing heat a non-stick *kadai* and roast onions for two minutes. Add *methi* and cook for another minute. Add mushrooms, stir and cook till all the water dries up. Add cottage cheese, salt and pepper powder. Mix well and set aside to cool.

2 In a bowl, mix together gram flour, soda bicarbonate, salt, red chilli powder, carom seeds, asafoetida, coriander leaves and sufficient water to make a batter of pouring consistency. Whisk well to ensure there are no lumps.

3 Heat a non-stick pan, pour a ladleful of batter into the pan and spread it evenly. Cook the *cheela* on both sides.

4 Place a portion of the stuffing in the centre, fold the edges over and serve immediately.

Veg | Preparation 10 mins | Cooking 15 mins | Serves 4 people

Corn *Bhel*

Stuffed Methi *Cheela*

INGREDIENTS

1 cup fresh corn kernels

1 large onion, finely chopped

1 large tomato, finely chopped

2 medium potatoes, boiled, cut into ½ inch cubes

2 teaspoons *chaat masala*

3-4 green chillies, finely chopped

2 tablespoons Green Coriander Chutney (pg. 32)

2 tablespoons Date and Tamarind Chutney (pg. 112)

4 tablespoons fresh coriander leaves, finely chopped

1½ teaspoons lemon juice

Salt to taste

1 cup cornflakes, crushed

Corn *Bhel*

1 Bring three cups of water to a boil. Add the corn kernels and continue to boil for three to four minutes. Drain and remove excess water. This *bhel* can be made with hot or cold corn kernels.

2 Mix together the corn, onion, tomato, potatoes, *chaat masala*, green chillies, green coriender chutney, date and tamarind chutney and coriander leaves. Add lemon juice, salt and toss to mix.

3 Divide into individual servings, sprinkle cornflakes and serve immediately.

Veg | Preparation 10 mins | Cooking 5 mins | Serves 4 people

Kathi Kebab

Rolls

INGREDIENTS

FOR KEBABS

500 grams mutton mince

¾ cup skimmed milk yogurt

1 tablespoon garlic paste

½ tablespoon ginger paste

1 teaspoon red chilli powder

½ teaspoon *garam masala* powder

Salt to taste

8 teaspoons Green Coriander Chutney (pg. 32)

4 teaspoons chilli sauce

4 teaspoons tomato sauce

2 medium onions, cut into rings

2 tablespoons lemon juice

2 teaspoons *chaat masala*

FOR THE ROTIS

1½ cups wholewheat flour (*atta*)

3 tablespoons skimmed milk yogurt

Salt to taste

1 Mix together yogurt, garlic paste, ginger paste, red chilli powder, *garam masala* powder and salt.

2 Marinate mutton mince in this marinade for about thirty to forty minutes.

3 Heat a non-stick pan. Add marinated mince and cook on moderate heat till the mince is cooked and dry. Divide into eight equal portions.

4 In another bowl mix together wholewheat flour, yogurt and salt. Add sufficient water and knead into a soft dough. Rest the dough for eight to ten minutes.

5 Divide dough into eight equal portions. Roll out each portion into *rotis* seven inches in diameter.

6 Roast *rotis* on a non-stick *tawa* till brown specks appear on both sides.

7 Spread a teaspoon of green coriander chutney on each *roti*, and drizzle with some chilli sauce and tomato sauce. Put a portion of mince, some onion rings and sprinkle with lemon juice and *chaat masala*. Roll up the *rotis* and serve immediately.

Non-Veg | Preparation 40 mins | Cooking 30 mins | Serves 4 people

Dahi
Idli

INGREDIENTS

1 cup parboiled rice (*ukda chawal*)

½ cup split black gram (*dhuli urad dal*)

Salt to taste

2 cups skimmed milk yogurt, whisked

6 tablespoons honey

2 tablespoons Green Coriander Chutney (pg. 32)

2 tablespoons Date and Tamarind Chutney (pg. 112)

¼ teaspoon red chilli powder

½ teaspoon cumin powder

2 tablespoons fresh coriander leaves, chopped

1. Wash rice and soak in three cups of water for at least two to three hours.
2. Wash and soak *dal* in two cups of water for the same length of time.
3. Drain and grind the rice to a slightly coarse texture. Use water as required to make a batter of dropping consistency. Drain and grind the *dal*, sprinkling water as required, to make a smooth and spongy batter.
4. Mix both the batters. Sprinkle salt and whip the mixture thoroughly with your fingers. Pour batter into a large vessel, close tightly with a lid and rest in a warm place overnight to ferment.
5. Heat sufficient water in a steamer.
6. Line the hollows of an *idli* stand with a piece of muslin. Pour a spoonful of the fermented batter into each hollow. Place the *idli* stand in the steamer. Steam for eight to ten minutes or till *idlis* are done.
7. Meanwhile, mix yogurt and honey thoroughly.
8. Place *idlis* in a serving bowl; drizzle sweetened yogurt, green coriander chutney and date and tamarind chutney over the *idlis*. Sprinkle red chilli powder and cumin powder.
9. Garnish with coriander leaves and serve.

Veg | Preparation 12 hrs | Cooking 15 mins | Serves 4 people

Paneer Frankie

INGREDIENTS

300 grams skimmed milk cottage cheese (*paneer*), ½ inch cubes

1 cup wholewheat flour (*atta*)

Salt to taste

3 medium onions, chopped

3 medium tomatoes, chopped

1 tablespoon ginger paste

1 tablespoon garlic paste

1 teaspoon Kashmiri red chilli powder

½ teaspoon turmeric powder

2 teaspoons coriander powder (optional)

2 tablespoons lemon juice

TO SERVE

8 teaspoons Green Coriander Chutney (pg. 32)

2 medium onions, sliced

1. Mix wholewheat flour and salt, add sufficient water and knead into a firm dough. Cover and rest the dough for about fifteen minutes.
2. Heat a non-stick pan, add onions, tomatoes, ginger paste, garlic paste, salt, Kashmiri red chilli powder, turmeric powder, coriander powder and stir well to mix. Cook till everything blends well and the excess moisture has dried up. Stir in the lemon juice, and take the pan off the heat.
3. Add *paneer* cubes and mix lightly. Divide the filling into eight equal portions and set aside.
4. Divide the dough into eight equal portions and roll into *rotis*.
5. Heat a *tawa* and cook each *roti* till both sides are evenly cooked.
6. Spread a teaspoonful of green coriander chutney over each *roti*. Place a portion of *paneer* mixture at one end. Sprinkle some sliced onions and roll up the *roti*.
7. Wrap in aluminium foil and serve immediately.

Veg | Preparation 15 mins | Cooking 15 mins | Serves 4 people

Paneer

Frankie

Vegetable Seekh

Kebabs

Vegetable Seekh *Kebabs*

INGREDIENTS

1 medium potato, boiled and mashed

1 medium carrot, grated

½ cup green peas, crushed

5-6 French beans, finely chopped

1 teaspoon ginger paste

1 teaspoon dried mango powder (*amchur*)

2 teaspoons *chaat masala*

3-4 green chillies, chopped

1½ tablespoons *chhunda*

3 tablespoons roasted *chana* powder

150 grams skimmed milk cottage cheese (*paneer*), grated

Salt to taste

1 Heat a non-stick *kadai*. Add ginger paste and cook for half a minute. Add mashed potato, carrot, green peas and French beans and cook for a few minutes, stirring continuously.

2 Add *amchur*, *chaat masala*, green chillies, *chhunda*, and roasted *chana* powder and continue to cook for two to three minutes.

3 Add cottage cheese and mix well. Add salt and mix again.

4 Divide into eight equal portions. Take each portion and press around a skewer in a cylindrical shape.

5 Heat a non-stick *tawa* and place the skewers on it. Cook on moderate heat, rotating the skewers from time to time so that the kebabs cook evenly all round, to a golden brown.

6 Serve hot with chutney of your choice.

Chef's Tip: *Chhunda is a sweet-sour pickle made of grated unripe green mangoes. A popular Gujarati accompaniment.*

Veg | Preparation 10 mins | Cooking 20 mins | Serves 4 people

Vegetable *Tacos*

INGREDIENTS

FOR THE TACOS

¼ cup maize flour (*makai ka atta*)

4 teaspoons refined flour (*maida*)

A small pinch of turmeric powder

Salt to taste

FOR THE FILLING

2 medium potatoes, peeled and quartered

½ cup green peas, shelled

5-6 French beans, strings removed

1 medium carrot, cut into four pieces

¼ teaspoon turmeric powder

Salt to taste

1 large onion, finely chopped

3-4 garlic cloves, finely chopped

1 teaspoon red chilli paste

2 tablespoons tomato ketchup

½ cup bean sprouts

1 head of lettuce, shredded

1. Mix all the ingredients for the tacos, add sufficient water and knead into a medium soft dough. Keep covered with a damp cloth for about fifteen minutes.
2. Divide into sixteen equal portions and roll into thin *puris*. Prick the *puris* with a fork.
3. Heat a non-stick *tawa*. Dry roast the *puris* on both sides. Fold over a rolling pin while still hot into a half-moon shape. Set aside to cool.
4. Boil potatoes, peas, French beans and carrot in sufficient water with turmeric powder and salt till done. When cooked, drain, mash and set aside to cool.
5. Heat a non-stick pan. Roast onion for two minutes. Add garlic and roast for another minute.
6. Add red chilli paste, salt and tomato ketchup. Cook for two minutes.
7. Add mashed vegetables and cook for another five to eight minutes. Take off the heat and cool.
8. To serve, stuff taco shells with the prepared filling. Top with bean sprouts and lettuce leaves. Serve immediately.

Veg | Preparation 15 mins | Cooking 30 mins | Serves 4 people

Masala Papad

INGREDIENTS

4 *urad dal papads*

1 medium onion, finely chopped

1 medium tomato, finely chopped

1 small green capsicum, seeded and finely chopped

4 tablespoons fresh coriander leaves, finely chopped

½ teaspoon red chilli powder

Salt to taste

1 teaspoon *chaat masala*

1 teaspoon lemon juice

1. Roast *papads* over a low flame or in a microwave oven.
2. Mix together onion, tomato, capsicum, half the fresh coriander leaves, red chilli powder and salt to taste.
3. Place each *papad* on a serving plate. Spread some onion-tomato mixture over it.
4. Sprinkle *chaat masala*, lemon juice and the remaining coriander leaves on top and serve immediately.

Veg | Preparation 10 mins | Cooking 5 mins | Serves 4 people

Hot Chilli Corn

INGREDIENTS

2 cups fresh corn kernels, boiled

1 teaspoon red chilli flakes

1 green chilli, chopped

1 tablespoon lemon juice

1 small green capsicum, seeded and chopped

1 small red capsicum, seeded and chopped

Salt to taste

3-4 black peppercorns, crushed

2 tablespoons fresh coriander leaves, chopped

1. Heat a non-stick pan. Add boiled corn kernels, red chilli flakes and green chilli and cook for a minute.
2. Add lemon juice, green capsicum, red capsicum and salt. Cover the pan and allow the vegetables to soften for about two minutes. Mix well.
3. Add crushed peppercorns and serve garnished with coriander leaves.

Veg | Preparation 10 mins | Cooking 5 mins | Serves 4 people

INGREDIENTS

200 grams prawns, peeled and deveined

1 teaspoon garlic paste

½ medium carrot

Salt to taste

7-8 black peppercorns, crushed

1 teaspoon lemon juice

2 teaspoons mustard paste

2 tablespoons tomato ketchup

10-15 garlic cloves, chopped

6-8 small onions, peeled

8 small broccoli florets

3-4 fresh basil leaves

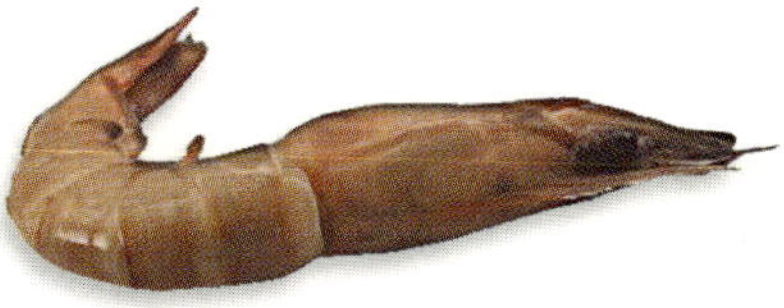

Roasted Garlic Prawns

1 Peel, wash and cut carrot into half-inch pieces. Put in sufficient boiling water and cook till nearly done. Drain and set aside.

2 Mix together garlic paste, salt, crushed peppercorns, lemon juice, mustard paste, tomato ketchup and garlic. Marinate prawns along with small onions, carrot and broccoli in this mixture for half an hour.

3 Heat a non-stick pan. Place marinated prawns and vegetables in it and cook for three to four minutes or till done. Alternatively, grill in a combi-microwave oven for three to four minutes.

4 Serve hot, garnished with roughly torn fresh basil leaves.

Non-Veg | Preparation 10 mins | Cooking 5 mins | Serves 4 people

Soya

Burger

Soya *Burger*

INGREDIENTS

1 cup soya granules

2½ cups skimmed milk

4-5 medium potatoes, boiled and mashed

1 medium onion, finely chopped

2 green chillies, finely chopped

2 tablespoons fresh coriander leaves, finely chopped

¼ teaspoon cumin powder

1 teaspoon red chilli powder

¼ teaspoon clove powder

¼ teaspoon cinnamon powder

1½ teaspoons lemon juice

Salt to taste

¾ cup brown breadcrumbs

TO SERVE

4 burger buns

4 tablespoons mustard paste

4 tablespoons tomato ketchup

10-12 lettuce leaves

1 medium onion, sliced into rings

1 Soak soya granules in two cups of milk for fifteen minutes. Drain and squeeze out excess milk. Grind to mince the granules further.

2 In a large mixing bowl, mix together soya granules, mashed potatoes, onion, green chillies, coriander leaves, cumin powder, red chilli powder, clove powder, cinnamon powder, lemon juice and salt.

3 Divide the mixture into four equal portions. Shape each portion into a patty of three inches diameter and about half an inch thick.

4 Coat each patty evenly with breadcrumbs.

5 Heat a non-stick pan and cook the patties on both sides till crisp.

6 Halve a burger bun horizontally. Apply mustard paste on the lower half and tomato ketchup on the top half. Place two or three lettuce leaves on the lower half. Place the patty on it, top with onion rings, cover with the top half of the bun and serve immediately.

Veg | Preparation 20 mins | Cooking 15 mins | Serves 4 people

INGREDIENTS

6 medium potatoes

1 medium onion, finely chopped

Salt to taste

7-8 black peppercorns, ground coarsely

A pinch of nutmeg powder

2 tablespoons fresh parsley, chopped

Hash Brown Potatoes

1. Boil potatoes in sufficient water till nearly done. They should be slightly undercooked.
2. Peel and grate potatoes.
3. Heat a non-stick pan. Add onion and roast till translucent. Remove from heat.
4. Preheat oven to 200°C/400°F/Gas Mark 6.
5. Mix grated potatoes and roasted onion along with salt, half the ground peppercorns and nutmeg powder.
6. Mix well and put in a baking tray and spread evenly with your fingers.
7. Sprinkle the remaining ground peppercorns over the potatoes.
8. Bake in the preheated oven for ten to fifteen minutes or till the potatoes turn light brown.
9. Cut into wedges, garnish with parsley and serve hot.

INGREDIENTS

300 grams boneless chicken breasts, cut into ½ inch pieces

1 inch ginger, finely sliced

3 garlic cloves, chopped

2-3 fresh red chillies, cut into thin strips

1 tablespoon soy sauce

1 teaspoon sugar

Salt to taste

15-16 black peppercorns, crushed

2 medium green capsicums, seeded and chopped

3 spring onions, chopped

Chicken and *Pepper Wraps*

1 Marinate chicken pieces with ginger, garlic, red chillies, soy sauce, sugar, salt, crushed black peppercorns, green capsicums and spring onions. Rest the marinated chicken for an hour, preferably in a refrigerator.

2 Cut four square pieces of aluminium foil measuring ten to twelve inches.

3 Divide the chicken mixture into four equal portions.

4 Place one portion of chicken mixture in the centre of each piece of aluminium foil. Fold in the open edges tightly so that the steam does not escape.

5 Place the parcels on a hot *tawa* and cook on medium heat for six to seven minutes. As the chicken gets cooked, the aluminium foil will puff up slightly.

6 Serve immediately in the foil.

Non-Veg | Preparation 1 hr | Cooking 15 mins | Serves 4 people

Chicken *Olivetti*

INGREDIENTS

- 4 (200 grams each) boneless chicken breasts
- 2 teaspoons ginger paste
- 2 teaspoons garlic paste
- ½ teaspoon black pepper powder
- 1 teaspoon soy sauce
- Salt to taste
- 2 tablespoons lemon juice
- ½ teaspoon red chilli flakes
- ½ teaspoon mixed herbs
- 12-16 green olives, stoned
- 2 medium tomatoes, 1½ inch pieces
- 7-8 black peppercorns, crushed
- 2-3 fresh parsley sprigs

1. Cut each chicken breast into one inch wide strips.
2. In a bowl mix ginger paste, garlic paste, pepper powder, soy sauce and salt. Add lemon juice and marinate the chicken pieces in this mixture.
3. Add red chilli flakes and mixed herbs and mix again. Rest for half an hour in a refrigerator.
4. Wrap a chicken strip around each olive and secure it with a toothpick. Reserve marinade.
5. Heat a non-stick pan and place the chicken olivettis on it. Cook, tossing the pieces occasionally, till chicken is almost done.
6. Add tomatoes mixed with reserved marinade. Stir and cook till the chicken is done. Add crushed black peppercorns and toss.
7. Arrange chicken olivettis on a plate and garnish with fresh parsley sprigs. Serve hot.

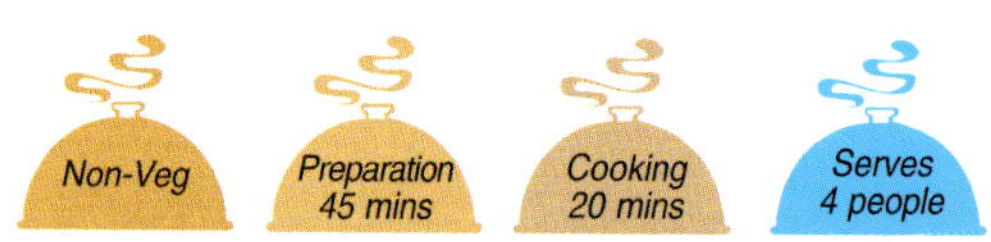

Chicken

Olivetti

Tandoori Stuffed Cauliflower

INGREDIENTS

2 small whole cauliflowers, trimmed

250 grams skimmed milk cottage cheese (*paneer*), grated

¼ teaspoon turmeric powder

1 tablespoon gram flour (*besan*)

2 cups drained skimmed milk yogurt

1 teaspoon dried fenugreek leaves (*kasoori methi*), roasted and crushed

2 teaspoons ginger paste

2 teaspoons garlic paste

1 teaspoon red chilli powder

1 teaspoon *chaat masala*

½ teaspoon *garam masala* powder

1 tablespoon lemon juice

Salt to taste

2 tablespoons raisins (*kishmish*)

¼ teaspoon carom seeds (*ajwain*)

2 tablespoons fresh mint leaves

4 tablespoons fresh coriander leaves, chopped

2-4 green chillies, finely chopped

1 lemon, cut into wedges

1 Boil five cups of water with a pinch of turmeric powder in a large pan. When the water starts to boil add whole cauliflowers. Boil for five minutes. Drain and refresh under running water.

2 Heat a non-stick pan and dry-roast *besan* on low heat till it gives out a pleasant aroma. Transfer into a bowl and set aside.

3 In a large bowl combine drained yogurt, roasted *besan*, *kasoori methi*, ginger paste, garlic paste, red chilli powder, remaining turmeric powder, half the *chaat masala*, *garam masala* powder, lemon juice and salt. Mix well and set aside.

4 Mix together *paneer*, raisins, carom seeds, mint leaves, half the chopped coriander leaves, remaining *chaat masala*, green chillies and salt.

5 Stuff the *paneer* mixture in between the florets of each cauliflower. Marinate the stuffed cauliflowers in the yogurt mixture for half an hour.

6 Preheat the oven to 200°C/400°F/Gas Mark 6.

7 Cook the cauliflowers in the preheated oven till done. Baste the cauliflowers with the reserved marinade from time to time.

8 Separate the cooked cauliflowers into florets and serve hot, garnished with lemon wedges and remaining coriander leaves.

Vegetable *Jhalfraizee*

INGREDIENTS

2 medium potatoes, ¼ inch thick oval slices

2 medium onions, halved and thickly sliced

2 medium green capsicums, seeded

1 large carrot

100 grams skimmed milk cottage cheese (*paneer*)

10 French beans

¼ small cauliflower, separated into florets

4 medium tomatoes

1 teaspoon cumin seeds

2 whole dried red chillies, broken into half

2 tablespoons vinegar

⅓ cup tomato ketchup

1½ teaspoons red chilli powder

½ teaspoon turmeric powder

2 inches ginger, cut into thin strips

Salt to taste

1 teaspoon *garam masala* powder

2 tablespoons fresh coriander leaves, chopped

1 Cut capsicum, carrot, paneer and French beans into fingers.

2 Blanch carrot and French beans in two cups of boiling water for two to three minutes. Drain and refresh in cold water. Blanch cauliflower florets in two cups of boiling water for three to four minutes. Drain and refresh.

3 Purée the tomatoes in a blender.

4 Heat a non-stick pan and roast cumin seeds and red chillies until the seeds change colour. Add vinegar and two tablespoons of water and cook till slightly reduced.

5 Add tomato purée and tomato ketchup and cook for two to three minutes.

6 Add red chilli powder, turmeric powder, ginger, potato slices, salt and one cup of water and cook for two to three minutes.

7 Add onions and capsicums and continue to cook for another two to three minutes.

8 Add carrot, French beans and cauliflower and toss. Add *paneer* and toss gently to mix.

9 Sprinkle *garam masala* powder and serve hot garnished with coriander leaves.

Veg | *Preparation 20 mins* | *Cooking 15 mins* | *Serves 4 people*

INGREDIENTS

3 large bunches (600 grams each) spinach, chopped

10-12 ears baby corn, cut into ½ inch pieces

2 medium onions, cut into 1 inch pieces

5-6 garlic cloves, chopped

2-3 green chillies, slit

1 medium green capsicum, seeded and cut into 1 inch pieces

2 tablespoons cornflour

¾ cup Vegetable Stock (pg.120)

Salt to taste

¼ teaspoon MSG (optional)

¼ teaspoon black pepper powder

Palak

Baby Corn Sabzi

1 Blanch the baby corn in two cups of boiling water for two to three minutes. Drain and set aside.

2 Heat a non-stick pan. Add onions and garlic and cook for two minutes.

3 Add green chillies, capsicum and baby corn and cook on high heat for two to three minutes.

4 Add spinach and toss. Add cornflour mixed with the vegetable stock and cook, stirring, for two to three minutes.

5 Stir in salt, MSG and pepper powder.

6 Serve hot.

Veg | Preparation 10 mins | Cooking 10 mins | Serves 4 people

Vegetable *Stew* *with Garlic Bread*

INGREDIENTS

2 medium carrots, cut into 1 inch pieces

¼ small cauliflower, separated into florets

¼ cup green peas, shelled

2 medium potatoes, cut into 1 inch pieces

1 medium zucchini, cut into 1 inch pieces

1 inch fresh ginger, sliced

3-4 cloves

8-10 black peppercorns

1 teaspoon cumin seeds

1 medium onion, sliced

$4^{1}/_{3}$ cups Vegetable Stock (pg. 120)

Salt to taste

1 stalk celery, cut into 1 inch pieces

3-4 black peppercorns, crushed

5 spinach leaves, shredded

1 loaf garlic bread, sliced

1 Blanch carrots, cauliflower and green peas individually in boiling water. Refresh in cold water and set aside.

2 Tie ginger, cloves, peppercorns and cumin seeds in a piece of muslin to make a *bouquet garni*.

3 Heat a non-stick pan. Add onion and roast lightly. Add vegetable stock and bring to a boil.

4 Put the *bouquet garni* into the boiling stock. Season with salt.

5 Add potatoes. Cover and cook over medium heat. Once the potatoes are cooked, remove the *bouquet garni* and mash the potatoes to thicken the stock.

6 Add celery, zucchini, carrots, cauliflower and green peas and cook on low heat for two minutes. Adjust salt and add crushed peppercorns.

7 Add spinach and mix well.

8 Lightly toast slices of garlic bread and serve with hot stew.

Veg | Preparation 20 mins | Cooking 20 mins | Serves 4 people

Chutneywale Aloo

Vegetable Stew *with Garlic Bread*

Chutneywale Aloo

INGREDIENTS

- 40 baby potatoes
- ½ teaspoon turmeric powder
- Salt to taste
- 1 cup fresh coriander leaves, roughly chopped
- ¼ cup fresh mint leaves, coarsely shredded
- 10-12 green chillies, coarsely chopped
- 4-6 garlic cloves, coarsely chopped
- 2 inches ginger, coarsely chopped
- 4 teaspoons lemon juice
- 2 teaspoons cumin seeds
- 2 teaspoons coriander powder
- 1 teaspoon cumin powder
- ½ cup skimmed milk yogurt
- 1 teaspoon sesame seeds (*til*), toasted

1 Parboil potatoes with salt and one-fourth teaspoon of turmeric powder. Drain, cool and halve without peeling.

2 For the chutney, grind coriander leaves, mint leaves, green chillies, garlic and ginger along with salt and lemon juice to a fine paste.

3 Heat a non-stick pan and dry roast cumin seeds till they emit a pleasant aroma. Add halved potatoes, coriander powder, cumin powder, remaining turmeric powder and mix well. Add half a cup of water, cover and cook on low heat till the potatoes are done.

4 Add the chutney, half a cup of water and stir to mix. Adjust salt and simmer for three to four minutes or till the gravy has thickened. Add yogurt and stir. Cook till the gravy comes to a boil and take off the heat.

5 Sprinkle toasted sesame seeds and serve hot.

Veg | Preparation 15 mins | Cooking 15 mins | Serves 4 people

Makai *Palak*

INGREDIENTS

½ cup corn kernels, boiled

2 large bunches (600 grams each) spinach

2 medium onions, chopped

1 inch fresh ginger, grated

2 green chillies, chopped

A pinch of turmeric powder

1 teaspoon red chilli powder

1 teaspoon dried mango powder (*amchur*)

Salt to taste

¼ cup skimmed milk yogurt

1 teaspoon *garam masala* powder

1 teaspoon dried fenugreek leaves (*kasoori methi*), crushed

1 inch fresh ginger, cut into thin strips

1 Blanch spinach in sufficient boiling water for one minute. Drain and purée in a blender.

2 Heat a non-stick pan and roast onions, ginger and green chillies for two to three minutes.

3 Add turmeric powder, red chilli powder, dried mango powder and salt. Add one-fourth cup of water. Mix well and simmer for one or two minutes.

4 Add yogurt and mix well. Add spinach purée, corn kernels and salt and cook for two minutes.

5 Add *garam masala* powder and *kasoori methi*, stir and remove from heat.

6 Garnish with ginger strips and serve hot with *rotis*.

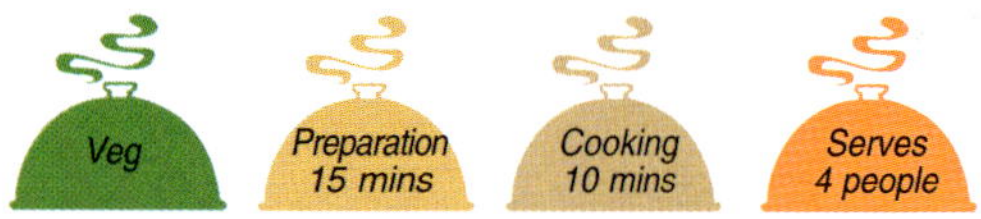

Masaledar Kaddu

INGREDIENTS

400 grams red pumpkin (*kaddu*)

½ teaspoon fenugreek seeds (*methi dana*)

A pinch of asafoetida

2 green chillies, chopped

Salt to taste

½ teaspoon turmeric powder

1 tablespoon coriander powder

1 inch ginger, cut into thin strips

1½ teaspoons red chilli powder

2 tablespoons sugar

1½ tablespoons lemon juice

2 tablespoons fresh coriander leaves, chopped

1 Peel the pumpkin and cut into one inch pieces.Heat a non-stick pan. Add fenugreek seeds, asafoetida, green chillies and pumpkin pieces and mix.

2 Add salt, turmeric powder, coriander powder, ginger and red chilli powder and mix. Add a little water, cover and cook on moderate heat for ten to fifteen minutes.

3 Add sugar, lemon juice and coriander leaves. Cover and cook on moderate heat for ten minutes till the pumpkin is very soft. Mash the pumpkin gently with the back of a spoon. Serve hot.

Veg | Preparation 15 mins | Cooking 20 mins | Serves 4 people

Tabbouleh *Stuffed* Tomatoes

INGREDIENTS

½ cup cracked wheat (burghul)

8 medium firm red tomatoes

2-3 spring onions, chopped

1 small radish, grated

2 tablespoons raisins (*kishmish*)

2 tablespoons lemon juice

Salt to taste

5-6 black peppercorns, crushed

3 tablespoons fresh parsley, chopped

6-8 lettuce leaves

6-8 fresh mint leaves

1 Soak the burghul in boiling hot water for half an hour. Drain, squeeze out excess water and set aside. Cut off the tops of the tomatoes and scoop out the seeds. Reserve the seeds.

2 Mix together burghul, spring onions, radish, raisins, lemon juice, salt, crushed peppercorns, parsley and reserved tomato seeds. Stuff the tomatoes with this filling. Heat sufficient water in a steamer.

3 Place stuffed tomatoes on a perforated plate in the steamer and steam for ten minutes. Remove and set aside to cool for a while. Serve warm, on a bed of lettuce, garnished with roughly torn mint leaves

Veg | Preparation 30 mins | Cooking 10 mins | Serves 4 people

Matar Paneer

INGREDIENTS

1 cup green peas, shelled

200 grams skimmed milk cottage cheese (*paneer*), cut into ½ inch cubes

¾ teaspoon cumin seeds

2 large onions, finely chopped

1 tablespoon ginger-garlic paste

2 green chillies, chopped

¼ teaspoon turmeric powder

1 teaspoon red chilli powder

1 teaspoon coriander powder

2 large tomatoes, puréed

Salt to taste

¼ teaspoon *garam masala* powder

1 tablespoon fresh coriander leaves, chopped

1 Heat a non-stick pan and add cumin seeds. When they begin to change colour, add onions and ginger-garlic paste. Cook till lightly browned. Add green chillies, turmeric powder, red chilli powder and coriander powder and one-third cup of water and mix well.

2 Add tomato purée, salt and one cup of water. Cook for two minutes. Add green peas and mix well. Cook for five minutes or till peas are done.

3 Add *paneer* cubes and *garam masala* powder and stir gently.

4 Serve hot garnished with coriander leaves.

Veg | Preparation 10 mins | Cooking 10 mins | Serves 4 people

Spinach

and Potato Bake

INGREDIENTS

2 large bunches (600 grams each) spinach

4 medium potatoes

4 medium onions

8-10 garlic cloves, chopped

Salt to taste

7-8 black peppercorns, crushed

½ teaspoon Tabasco sauce

¾ cup skimmed milk

A pinch of nutmeg powder

½ cup brown breadcrumbs

1 Blanch spinach in sufficient boiling water for one minute. Drain, refresh in cold water and chop.

2 Boil two potatoes, peel and mash till smooth. Peel and slice the remaining two potatoes into thin slices. Blanch in hot water for two to three minutes, drain and set aside. Chop two onions and slice the remaining two into rings.

3 Preheat the oven to 180°C/350°F/Gas Mark 4.

4 Heat a non-stick pan and roast chopped onions and garlic till light brown. Add spinach (first press it with your hands to remove excess water). Cook for a few minutes till all the water is absorbed. Add salt, half the crushed peppercorns and Tabasco sauce. Set aside.

5 Heat another non-stick pan. Toss the potato slices and onion rings together. Add salt and remaining crushed peppercorns and toss again.

6 Mix the mashed potatoes, milk and nutmeg powder together to a smooth mixture. Transfer into a piping bag with a star nozzle.

7 Take an ovenproof dish and layer the spinach mixture and potato and onion mixture in alternate layers. Sprinkle the breadcrumbs over the last layer. Pipe mashed potato rosettes on top and bake for thirty minutes. Serve hot.

Veg | Preparation 20 mins | Cooking 40 mins | Serves 4 people

Thai Green Curry with Vegetables

Main Course

Thai Green

Curry with Vegetables

INGREDIENTS

1 medium carrot, cut into diamonds

½ small cauliflower, separated into small florets

2-3 baby brinjals

1 medium potato, cut into ½ inch cubes

5 stalks lemon grass

1 teaspoon lemon juice

Salt to taste

¾ cup fresh coconut milk

2-3 fresh basil leaves

GREEN CURRY PASTE

10 green chillies

3 shallots/*sambhar* onions

9 garlic cloves

1 inch galangal

3 inch stalk lemon grass

¼ teaspoon lemon rind, grated

A small bunch of coriander roots

2 teaspoons coriander seeds

2 teaspoons cumin seeds

Salt to taste

1 To make green curry paste, grind green chillies, shallots, garlic, galangal, lemon grass, lemon rind, coriander roots, coriander seeds, cumin seeds and salt to a fine paste.

2 Blanch all the vegetables individually in boiling water and refresh in cold water. Tie lemon grass in a piece of muslin to make a bundle. Crush it slightly.

3 Heat a non-stick pan, add green curry paste and roast for one minute. Add the blanched vegetables and lemon juice and cook for three to four minutes, stirring continuously.

4 Add three cups of water and continue to cook. Add lemon grass bundle and cook for three to four minutes till the curry absorbs its flavour.

5 Remove the lemon grass and add salt and coconut milk. Simmer for one minute.

6 Add basil leaves and take off the heat. Serve hot.

Chef's Tip: *Galangal is a type of ginger used in Thai cooking. If not available use ginger.*

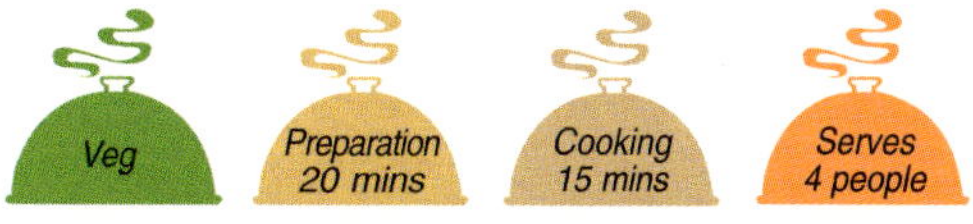

INGREDIENTS

- 20 unpeeled baby potatoes
- ½ cup skimmed milk yogurt
- A pinch of asafoetida
- 2 teaspoons garlic paste
- 2 teaspoons ginger paste
- 2 teaspoons red chilli powder
- ½ teaspoon turmeric powder
- 2 teaspoons coriander powder
- 1 teaspoon cumin powder
- ½ teaspoon *garam masala* powder
- Salt to taste
- 2 large onions, chopped
- 2 tablespoons fresh coriander leaves, chopped

Baby Potatoes

in Spicy Yogurt Gravy

1 Parboil potatoes in sufficient water. Drain and set aside.

2 Mix together yogurt, asafoetida, garlic paste, ginger paste, red chilli powder, turmeric powder, coriander powder, cumin powder, *garam masala* powder and salt. Pierce unpeeled baby potatoes with a fork, add to the marinade and marinate for about half an hour.

3 Heat a non-stick pan and roast onions till lightly browned. Add baby potatoes along with the marinade and mix. Once the mixture comes to a boil, lower the heat and cook till the gravy thickens and coats the potatoes.

4 Garnish with coriander leaves and serve hot with *rotis*.

Veg | *Preparation 30 mins* | *Cooking 10 mins* | *Serves 4 people*

INGREDIENTS

1 cup soya granules

1 cup shelled green peas

1½ cups skimmed milk

2 medium onions, finely chopped

8 garlic cloves, finely chopped

1 inch ginger, grated

2 green chillies, chopped

1 teaspoon coriander powder

1 teaspoon cumin powder

¾ teaspoon red chilli powder

4 tablespoons fresh coriander leaves, chopped

Salt to taste

1 teaspoon *garam masala* powder

1 tablespoon lemon juice

Soya Keema *Matar*

1 Soak soya granules in milk for an hour. Heat a non-stick pan and add onions. Roast till lightly browned. Add garlic and roast for a minute. Add ginger, green chillies, coriander powder, cumin powder, red chilli powder and two tablespoons of water. Stir and cook for two minutes.

2 Add green peas and one-fourth cup of water and mix well. Cover and cook till peas are nearly done. Add soya granules along with the milk and cook till almost dry.

3 Add coriander leaves, salt, *garam masala* powder and lemon juice and mix well. Serve hot.

Veg | Preparation 60 mins | Cooking 20 mins | Serves 4 people

Soya Keema

Matar

Gatta

Curry

INGREDIENTS

FOR THE GATTA

- 2½ cups gram flour (*besan*), sifted
- 3 tablespoons skimmed milk yogurt
- ½ teaspoon cumin seeds
- ½ teaspoon red chilli powder
- ½ teaspoon turmeric powder
- Salt to taste
- A pinch of soda bi-carbonate

FOR THE GRAVY

- 2 medium onions
- ½ inch ginger
- 1½ cups skimmed milk yogurt
- 1 teaspoon red chilli powder
- 2 teaspoons coriander powder
- ½ teaspoon turmeric powder
- 1 teaspoon cumin seeds
- A pinch of asafoetida
- Salt to taste
- ½ teaspoon *garam masala* powder
- 2 tablespoons fresh coriander leaves, chopped

Gatta

Curry

1. Mix all the ingredients for the *gatta*. Add sufficient water to make a stiff dough. Divide into six equal portions and roll into cylindrical shapes.
2. Cook the *gatta* in five cups of boiling hot water for ten to fifteen minutes. Drain and reserve the water for the gravy. Cut *gatta* diagonally into one inch pieces.
3. Roughly cut onions and boil in half a cup of water. Cool and grind with ginger to a fine paste.
4. Whisk yogurt with red chilli powder, coriander powder and turmeric powder.
5. Heat a non-stick pan. Add cumin seeds and asafoetida. Roast until cumin seeds start to change colour.
6. Add onion paste and cook on low heat till it turns light pink.
7. Add yogurt mixture and simmer for five minutes.
8. Add *gatta*, salt and one cup of the reserved water in which *gatta* were boiled. Simmer till gravy thickens. Add *garam masala* powder and adjust seasoning.
9. Garnish with coriander leaves and serve hot.

Veg | Preparation 15 mins | Cooking 30 mins | Serves 4 people

Steamed *Lauki* and *Palak Koftas*

INGREDIENTS

FOR THE *KOFTA*

1 small (250 grams) bottle gourd (*lauki*), peeled and grated

2 medium bunches (350 grams each) spinach

Salt to taste

3 medium potatoes, boiled and mashed

2-3 green chillies, finely chopped

1 tablespoon raisins (*kishmish*)

3 tablespoons coarse rice powder

½ teaspoon *chaat masala*

1 teaspoon ginger paste

1 teaspoon garlic paste

1 large onion, finely chopped

FOR THE CURRY

1 teaspoon ginger paste

1 teaspoon garlic paste

1 large onion, chopped

1 teaspoon red chilli powder

¼ teaspoon turmeric powder

½ teaspoon *garam masala* powder

1 teaspoon dried fenugreek leaves (*kasoori methi*), roasted and crushed

5-6 medium tomatoes, puréed

1½ tablespoons honey

2 tablespoons fresh coriander leaves, chopped

1 Add salt to the grated bottle gourd and leave for five minutes. Squeeze bottle gourd to completely remove excess water. Blanch spinach in sufficient boiling water for one minute. Drain, refresh in cold water, squeeze out excess water and chop.

2 Combine the bottle gourd and spinach with potatoes, green chillies, raisins, rice powder, *chaat masala*, ginger paste, garlic paste, onion and salt in a large bowl. Divide into twenty equal portions and shape into oval *koftas*. Steam the *koftas* in a steamer for fifteen-twenty minutes. Set aside.

3 Heat a non-stick pan. Roast ginger paste, garlic paste and onion on medium heat for five to six minutes. Add red chilli powder, turmeric powder, *garam masala* powder, *kasoori methi* and two tablespoons of water and cook for a minute.

4 Add tomato purée, honey and salt. Add one cup of water and simmer for ten minutes. Arrange the steamed *koftas* on a serving plate, pour the gravy over and serve immediately garnished with coriander leaves.

Veg | Preparation 15 mins | Cooking 30 mins | Serves 4 people

Mixed Sprouts

Ussal

INGREDIENTS

1 cup mixed sprouts (such as *moong, matki, chana*)

½ teaspoon mustard seeds

6-8 curry leaves

2 medium onions, finely chopped

½ teaspoon turmeric powder

½ teaspoon red chilli powder

1 teaspoon *Goda Masala* Powder (pg. 120)

1 teaspoon jaggery, grated

Salt to taste

2 tablespoons fresh coriander leaves, finely chopped

2 tablespoons scraped coconut

FOR THE SPICE PASTE

6-7 garlic cloves

3-4 green chillies, roughly chopped

1 teaspoon cumin seeds, roasted

¼ cup scraped coconut

1 For the spice paste, grind garlic, green chillies, cumin seeds and scraped coconut to a smooth paste using little water if required.

2 Heat a non-stick pan, add mustard seeds and when they crackle add curry leaves and onions. Cook, stirring continuously till onions turn light golden.

3 Add ground paste and cook on moderate heat for three to four minutes.

4 Add turmeric powder, red chilli powder, *goda masala*, jaggery and salt. Stir well.

5 Add mixed sprouts, stir and add enough water to just cover the sprouts.

6 Bring to a boil and continue cooking on moderate heat, stirring occasionally, till the sprouts are cooked.

7 Serve hot garnished with coriander leaves and coconut.

Veg | Preparation 10 mins | Cooking 15 mins | Serves 4 people

Main Course

INGREDIENTS

40 (400 grams) fresh button mushrooms, quartered

10-12 spring onions, chopped

5 stalks spring onion green, sliced diagonally

12 garlic cloves, finely chopped

1 tablespoon rice flour

1 cup skimmed milk yogurt, whisked

3 cloves

3 green chillies, seeded and chopped

2 teaspoons coriander powder

Salt to taste

½ teaspoon red chilli powder

½ teaspoon turmeric powder

Khumb

Hara Pyaaz

1 Heat a non-stick pan, add garlic and roast for a minute. Add mushrooms and continue cooking for three to four minutes on low heat. Add rice flour and mix.

2 Add yogurt and cook till the mixture thickens.

3 Add cloves, spring onions and green chillies and continue to cook on low heat for two minutes.

4 Add coriander powder, salt, red chilli powder, turmeric powder and half a cup of water.

5 Cook for two to three minutes. Stir in the spring onion greens. Serve hot.

Veg | Preparation 10 mins | Cooking 15 mins | Serves 4 people

Khumb Hara

Pyaaz

Jacket Potatoes with Baked Beans Stuffing

INGREDIENTS

4 large potatoes

1 cup baked beans

1 bay leaf

1 medium onion, chopped

6 garlic cloves, chopped

1 tablespoon tomato ketchup

1 teaspoon sea salt

¼ teaspoon black pepper powder

1. Parboil potatoes with the skins on. Drain, cool and halve. Scoop out the centres leaving a thick shell around.
2. Preheat the oven to 200°C/400°F/Gas Mark 6.
3. Heat a non-stick pan, add bay leaf, onion and garlic and cook till the onion turns a light brown.
4. Add tomato ketchup and mix well.
5. Add baked beans, sea salt and pepper powder, stir and bring the mixture to a boil.
6. Cool slightly. Fill the scooped out potato halves with the baked beans mixture. Arrange the potatoes on a baking tray and bake for fifteen to twenty minutes.
7. Serve hot.

Note: *The scooped out portion of the potatoes can be used in some other dish.*

Veg | Preparation 15 mins | Cooking 30 mins | Serves 4 people

Middle *Eastern* *Vegetable* Stew

INGREDIENTS

2 medium potatoes, peeled, cut into 1 inch cubes

2 medium carrots, peeled, cut into 1 inch cubes

1 green capsicum, seeded, cut into 1 inch pieces

2 medium zucchini, cut into 1 inch pieces

1 small bunch spinach, chopped

½ cup chickpeas (*Kabuli chana*)

3 cups Vegetable Stock (pg. 120)

1 inch fresh ginger, sliced

3-4 cloves

8-10 black peppercorns

1 stalk celery, cut into 1 inch pieces

1 teaspoon cumin powder

A pinch of red chilli powder

Salt to taste

½ teaspoon black pepper powder

10 fresh mint leaves

1. Wash and soak chickpeas in sufficient water overnight or for at least six hours. Pressure cook till done and set aside.

2. Heat vegetable stock in a saucepan and bring to a boil.

3. Tie ginger slices, cloves and peppercorns in a piece of muslin and add to the boiling stock.

4. Add boiled chickpeas, potatoes, carrots, celery, cumin powder and red chilli powder. Mix well and cook on medium heat till it begins to boil.

5. Cover and simmer on low heat till all the vegetables are cooked and tender. Add the capsicum, zucchini and spinach and cook for two minutes. Remove the spice bundle and discard.

6. Season with salt and pepper powder and garnish with mint leaves. Serve hot.

Veg | Preparation 15 mins | Cooking 30 mins | Serves 4 people

INGREDIENTS

4 pomfrets (200 grams each)

Salt to taste

2 tablespoons lemon juice

½ teaspoon turmeric powder

2-3 banana leaves

2 lemons, cut into wedges

2 medium onions, cut into rings

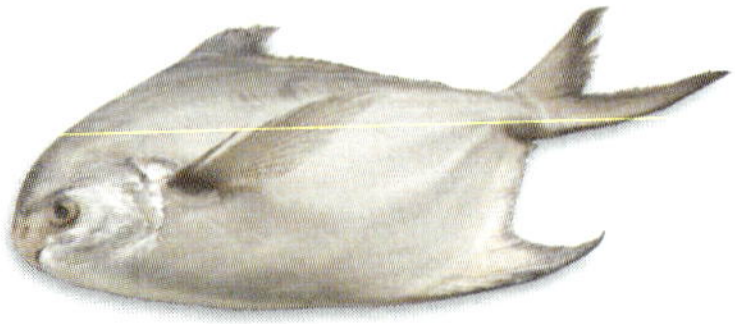

FOR THE *MASALA* PASTE

6 whole dried red chillies

2 teaspoons coriander seeds

2 teaspoons cumin seeds

5-6 black peppercorns

4-5 cloves

½ inch cinnamon

8 garlic cloves

1 inch ginger

1 medium tomato, coarsely chopped

2 tablespoons vinegar

½ teaspoon sugar

Salt to taste

Baked Fish *in Red Masala*

1 Wash, clean and pat the fish dry. Make diagonal slits on either sides of the fish using a sharp knife. Rub salt, lemon juice and turmeric powder well over the fish. Set aside for half an hour, preferably in a refrigerator.

2 Combine all the ingredients for the *masala* and grind to a smooth paste, using a little water if required.

3 Apply the paste on both the sides of the fish and set aside for fifteen minutes, preferably in a refrigerator.

4 Pre-heat the oven to 200ºC/400ºF/Gas Mark 6.

5 Wrap fish in banana leaves and place on a baking tray and bake for ten to fifteen minutes.

6 Serve hot with lemon wedges and onion rings.

Non-Veg | Preparation 45 mins | Cooking 20 mins | Serves 4 people

Goan Fish Curry

INGREDIENTS

2 pomfrets (400 grams each) or any flat fish

1 small onion, chopped

2 green chillies, slit and halved

Salt to taste

1 tablespoon malt vinegar

FOR THE SPICE PASTE

2 teaspoons cumin seeds

2 tablespoons coriander seeds

6 whole dried red chillies

½ cup scraped coconut

2 inches ginger, coarsely chopped

15 garlic cloves, coarsely chopped

1 tablespoon tamarind pulp

1 Cut each pomfret into six slices. Dry roast cumin seeds, coriander seeds and whole red chillies.

2 Make a fine paste of all the roasted spices along with coconut, ginger, garlic and tamarind with a little water.

3 Apply half the ground paste to the fish.

4 Heat a non-stick pan. Add onions and roast till light brown. Add green chillies. Cook on medium heat for three minutes, stirring constantly.

5 Add the remaining ground paste and stir well. Cook for three minutes, on low heat, till it emits a pleasant aroma. Add one and a half cups of water and bring to a boil. Add the marinated fish and salt. Cook on low heat for about five minutes or till fish is just done.

6 Stir in vinegar and serve hot with steamed rice.

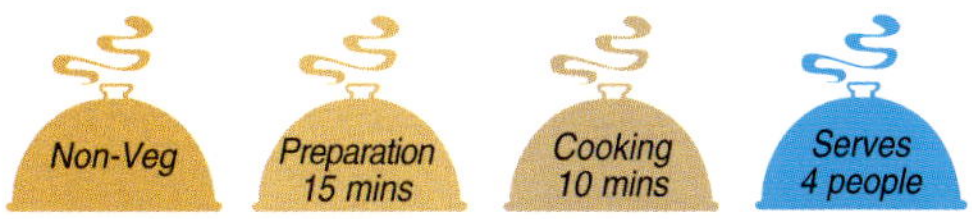

Daab

Chingri

Daab Chingri

INGREDIENTS

1 cup small prawns, peeled and deveined

1 small tender coconut (*daab*)

2 medium onions, finely sliced

4-5 green chillies, slit

¼ cup scraped coconut

1 teaspoon ginger paste

1½ teaspoons garlic paste

Salt to taste

¼ teaspoon turmeric powder

¼ cup tender coconut flesh (*malai*), chopped

½ teaspoon *paanch phoron*

wholewheat flour *(atta)* dough, as required

1. Take a tender coconut (*daab*), cut off a slice from the top, drain the water and scoop out the flesh; retain the top to use as a lid.
2. Wash prawns thoroughly under running water. Drain completely.
3. Preheat the oven to 220°C/425°F/Gas Mark 7.
4. In a bowl mix prawns, onions, green chillies, coconut, ginger paste, garlic paste, salt, turmeric powder and tender coconut flesh.
5. Heat a non-stick pan. Add *panch phoron* and when the seeds crackle, add to the mixture.
6. Fill the *daab* with the mixture.
7. Cover the *daab* using the reserved top slice. Seal the top with atta dough.
8. Bake for approximately thirty minutes. Let it stand for ten more minutes.
9. Open the seal just before serving.

Note: *Paanch phoran is a mixture of equal quantities of five spices : mustard seeds, fenugreek seeds, fennel seeds, cumin seeds and onion seeds. It is used extensively in Bengali cooking.*

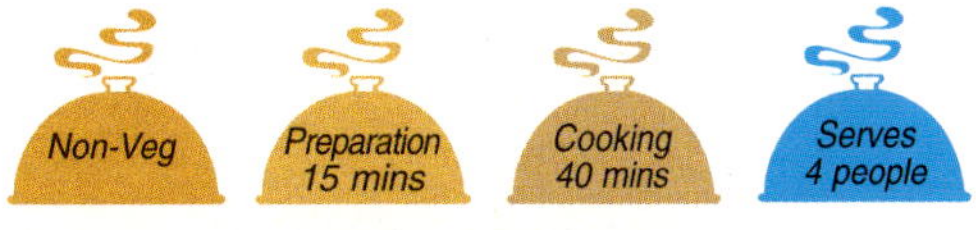

Fish

in Tomato Pepper Sauce

INGREDIENTS

1 (600-700 grams) King fish (*surmai*)

2 tablespoons lemon juice

½ teaspoon dried oregano

1 teaspoon dried basil

Salt to taste

15-16 black peppercorns, crushed

2-3 garlic cloves, chopped

FOR THE SAUCE

6 garlic cloves, chopped

1 medium onion, chopped

2 cups tomato concassé (see below)

½ cup white wine (optional)

3 tablespoons tomato ketchup

1. Fillet the fish and cut into four steaks.
2. Combine lemon juice, half the oregano, basil, salt, peppercorns and garlic and smear the fish steaks with the paste. Set aside to marinate for twenty to thirty minutes.
3. In a non-stick frying pan roast garlic and onion till brown. Add tomato concassé, remaining oregano, white wine and tomato ketchup and cook for a couple of minutes.
4. Add marinated fish steaks. Cover and cook till done.
5. Serve hot.

Note: *For Tomato Concassé, blanch tomatoes in sufficient boiling water for two minutes. Drain, refresh in cold water, peel, cut, remove seeds and chop.*

Non-Veg | Preparation 30 mins | Cooking 10 mins | Serves 4 people

Chilli Garlic Prawns

INGREDIENTS

16-20 medium prawns (400 grams), peeled and deveined

3 medium tomatoes, chopped

Salt to taste

1 inch ginger, cut into thin strips

2 tablespoons fresh coriander leaves, chopped

SPICE PASTE

1 inch ginger, coarsely chopped

10-12 garlic cloves, coarsely chopped

6-8 whole dried red chillies, seeded

¼ teaspoon turmeric powder

1½ teaspoons cumin seeds

1 Grind the ginger, garlic, red chilies, turmeric powder and cumin seeds to a fine paste. Heat a non-stick pan. Add tomatoes, ground spice paste and salt and cook for three to four minutes on moderate heat till the paste is almost dry.

2 Add prawns and cook till done. Serve hot garnished with ginger strips and coriander leaves.

Non-Veg
Preparation 10 mins
Cooking 10 mins
Serves 4 people

Steamed Fish

INGREDIENTS

2 medium fillets of King fish (*surmai*) (400 grams)

1 inch ginger, sliced

6-8 garlic cloves, crushed

2-3 green chillies, slit

Salt to taste

2 tablespoons lemon juice

2-3 lemon slices

6-8 sprigs fresh coriander leaves

1 medium carrot, grated

¼ medium cabbage, shredded

1 Cut each fish fillet into two pieces.

2 Place fish in a clay pot. Add ginger, garlic, green chillies, salt, lemon juice and mix.

3 Add lemon slices and half a cup of water. Cover and bring to a boil. Reduce heat and cook for about four minutes.

4 Chop the coriander leaves along with their stems and add them together with carrot and cabbage to the boiling fish. Cover once again and cook for one minute. Serve hot.

Non-Veg
Preparation 10 mins
Cooking 10 mins
Serves 4 people

Fish in *Banana Leaves*

INGREDIENTS

4 fillets of pomfret, (400 grams)

Salt to taste

4 tablespoons lemon juice

1 cup fresh coriander leaves

4 green chillies

½ cup scraped coconut

3 teaspoons cumin seeds

6-8 garlic cloves

3-4 banana leaves

1. Clean, wash and cut fish fillets into two inch by one-and-a-half inch pieces.
2. Sprinkle salt and half of the lemon juice and set aside for half an hour.
3. Grind coriander leaves, green chillies, coconut, cumin seeds and garlic to a fine paste. Add salt and remaining lemon juice to it. Mix well.
4. Apply this marinade to fish fillets and marinate for at least fifteen minutes.
5. Cut banana leaves into four pieces each.
6. Put one marinated piece of fish on each piece of banana leaf along with a little of the marinade and fold the leaves to seal tightly.
7. Steam the fish in a steamer for fifteen minutes and serve hot.

Non-Veg | Preparation 30 mins | Cooking 15 mins | Serves 4 people

Fish in Banana *Leaves*

Grilled Fish *with Salsa*

INGREDIENTS

8 King fish (*surmai*) darnes

Salt to taste

3 tablespoons lemon juice

2 tablespoons malt vinegar

2 tablespoons English mustard paste

1 tablespoon ginger-garlic paste

1 tablespoon red chilli sauce

16 cloves

FOR THE SALSA

½ cup corn kernels

10-12 fresh basil leaves

1 large onion, roasted and chopped

4-5 garlic cloves, roasted and finely chopped

2 medium tomatoes, chopped

2 canned pineapple slices, chopped

1 jalapeno pepper, finely chopped

Salt to taste

1 tablespoon lemon juice

2 tablespoons fresh coriander leaves, finely chopped

1 Marinate fish darnes in salt, lemon juice, malt vinegar, English mustard paste, ginger-garlic paste and red chilli sauce for half an hour.

2 Preheat the grill.

3 Stud marinated darnes with cloves, place them under the hot grill and cook for eight to ten minutes (or until fish flakes easily with a fork) turning once. Do not overcook the fish. Remove cloves.

4 To make the salsa, boil corn kernels with one cup of water for two to three minutes; drain. You can also cook them on Microwave HIGH (100%) for one minute.

5 Tear basil leaves roughly reserving a few to garnish. Mix together corn, onion, garlic, tomatoes, pineapple, jalapeno pepper, salt, basil leaves, lemon juice and coriander leaves.

6 To serve: spread salsa on a plate. Place grilled fish on it and garnish with reserved basil leaves.

Note: *Darnes are thick slices of fish cut on the bone.*

Chef's Tip: *Jalapeno peppers belong to the capsicum family. These peppers are very pungent and are used extensively in Mexican cooking.*

Non-Veg | Preparation 15 mins | Cooking 15 mins | Serves 4 people

Chicken and Rice *Bake*

INGREDIENTS

2 cups chicken mince

1 cup Basmati rice

1 teaspoon dried thyme

4-6 black peppercorns

Salt to taste

2 bay leaves

2 medium onions, halved

4 medium tomatoes, halved

10-12 garlic cloves, chopped

20 black peppercorns, crushed

3-4 leaves fresh basil

1½ cups Tomato Concassé (pg. 78)

3 tablespoons fresh brown breadcrumbs

1 teaspoon fresh parsley, chopped

1. Soak rice in three cups of water for half an hour. Drain and set aside.

2. Boil three cups of water in a deep pan, add thyme, black peppercorns, salt and bay leaves. Add soaked rice and cook till the rice is three-fourths done. Drain excess water and set aside.

3. Place onions and tomatoes along with garlic on a baking tray and cook in the oven till charred. Cool and chop roughly.

4. Heat a non-stick pan, add the chicken mince and keep stirring till the juices have completely evaporated.

5. Add roasted onions, tomatoes and garlic along with salt and crushed black peppercorns and mix well. Cover the pan and cook for a minute.

6. Once the mince is cooked, tear basil leaves with your fingers and add to the mince. Mix well.

7. Preheat the oven to 200°C/400°F/Gas Mark 6.

8. In a casserole or baking dish, arrange layers of half the tomato concassé, half the rice and half the chicken. Repeat the layers. Finally top with fresh breadcrumbs and bake for fifteen minutes.

9. Take out of the oven when breadcrumbs are a light golden brown. Garnish with parsley and serve immediately.

Non-Veg | Preparation 30 mins | Cooking 45 mins | Serves 4 people

Burghul-crusted Chicken

INGREDIENTS

- 4 boneless chicken breasts with skin, (200 grams each)
- 1½ cup cracked wheat (burghul)
- 2 egg whites
- ¼ tablespoon wholewheat flour (*atta*)
- Salt to taste
- 3-4 black peppercorns, crushed

FOR THE MARINADE

- 2 medium onions, chopped
- 10 garlic cloves, chopped
- 1 celery stalk, chopped
- ½ teaspoon red chilli powder
- 2 tablespoons soy sauce
- 1 tablespoon vinegar
- Salt to taste
- 3-4 black peppercorns, crushed

FOR THE SAUCE

- 4 medium tomatoes, blanched and puréed
- 8 garlic cloves, chopped
- 2 medium onions, chopped
- 4 tablespoons tomato ketchup
- Salt to taste
- 3-4 black peppercorns, crushed
- ½ teaspoon dried oregano

1 Boil five cups of water. Take off the heat and add burghul. After half a minute drain the burghul and tie up in a piece of muslin to drain. When completely dry empty onto a plate. To make the marinade, combine onions, garlic, celery, red chilli powder, soy sauce, vinegar, salt and crushed peppercorns. Add chicken breasts and marinate for an hour, preferably in the refrigerator. Preheat oven to 200°C/400°F/Gas Mark 6.

2 Whisk egg whites, wholewheat flour, salt and crushed peppercorns together to make a smooth batter. Dip chicken breasts in the batter, then roll them in burghul. Press lightly.

3 Heat a non-stick pan and place the chicken breasts on it. Cook on high heat for half a minute on each side to seal the juices. Transfer to a baking tray and bake for ten minutes or till done.

4 To make the sauce, blanch tomatoes in sufficient boiling water for two minutes. Drain, peel and purée. Heat another non-stick pan. Add garlic and onion and cook till the onion turns translucent. Add tomato purée and tomato ketchup and bring the mixture to a boil.

5 Add one and one-fourth cups of water and cook for eight to ten minutes till it reaches the consistency of a sauce. Add salt, crushed peppercorns, and oregano and stir to mix. Place chicken breasts on a serving plate, pour the sauce over and serve hot.

Non-Veg | Preparation 20 mins | Cooking 30 mins | Serves 4 people

INGREDIENTS

450 grams boneless chicken, cut into 1 inch cubes

2 teaspoons cumin seeds

2 teaspoons coriander seeds

5-6 black peppercorns

2-3 cloves

4 tablespoons fresh coriander leaves

2 tablespoons fresh mint leaves

½ inch ginger

8-10 garlic cloves

2-3 green chillies

1 cup skimmed milk yogurt, drained

Salt to taste

1 teaspoon *garam masala* powder

1 lemon, cut into wedges

Chutney Chicken

1 Dry roast cumin seeds, coriander seeds, peppercorns and cloves. Cool slightly and grind along with coriander leaves, mint leaves, ginger, garlic and green chillies to a fine paste.

2 In a bowl mix yogurt, salt and *garam masala* powder with the ground paste and marinate the chicken pieces in this mixture for an hour, preferably in a refrigerator.

3 Heat a non-stick pan, add the marinated chicken, cover and cook, stirring now and then, till the chicken is cooked and the gravy has thickened.

4 Serve hot with lemon wedges.

Non-Veg | Preparation 60 mins | Cooking 20 mins | Serves 4 people

Honey and *Orange Glazed Chicken*

INGREDIENTS

4 boneless chicken breasts, (200 grams each)

1 inch ginger, chopped

Salt to taste

2 tablespoons mustard paste

6 tablespoons orange juice

3-4 black peppercorns, crushed

1 teaspoon red chilli flakes

4 tablespoons honey

2 tablespoons lemon juice

8-10 baby onions, peeled

2 medium carrots, thickly sliced

FOR THE GLAZE

1 cup orange juice

½ teaspoon red chilli flakes

2 tablespoons honey

2 teaspoons mustard paste

1 In a bowl mix ginger, salt, mustard paste, orange juice, crushed black peppercorns, red chilli flakes, honey and lemon juice. Marinate the chicken in this mixture for about an hour.

2 Preheat the oven to 200°C/400°F/Gas Mark 6.

3 Heat a non-stick pan. Add baby onions and carrots and roast for two minutes.

4 Spread the vegetables in a baking tray. Arrange the marinated chicken with the marinade on the vegetables. Cook in the oven till done.

5 Meanwhile, for the glaze, mix orange juice, red chilli flakes, honey and mustard paste and cook in a non-stick pan till reduced to half the original quantity.

6 Mid-way through the baking, glaze the chicken with this mixture and continue to bake till the chicken is cooked. Serve hot.

Non-Veg | Preparation 60 mins | Cooking 30 mins | Serves 4 people

Honey and Orange Glazed Chicken

INGREDIENTS

1 whole chicken (800 grams), 8 pieces on the bone

¼ small bunch fresh fenugreek leaves (*methi*), chopped

1 cup skimmed milk yogurt, whisked

Salt to taste

4 one inch pieces of ginger

5 green cardamoms

1 black cardamom

5 cloves

1 inch cinnamon

1 bay leaf

1-2 blades mace (*javitri*)

2 large onions, chopped

20 garlic cloves, chopped

3 green chillies, seeded and chopped

½ teaspoon turmeric powder

1 teaspoon coriander power

1 teaspoon red chilli powder

2 medium tomatoes, chopped

1 tablespoon dried fenugreek leaves (*kasoori methi*)

¼ cup fresh coriander leaves, chopped

Methi Murgh

1. Mix together yogurt and salt in a large bowl. Add chicken and marinate for about half an hour. Chop half the ginger and cut the rest into thin strips.

2. Heat a non-stick pan, add green cardamoms, black cardamom, cloves, cinnamon, bay leaf and mace and roast over medium heat till fragrant.

3. Add onions and cook till they turn golden brown. Add garlic, chopped ginger and green chillies and cook for two minutes.

4. Add turmeric powder, coriander powder, red chilli powder and one-fourth cup of water. Stir and cook for half a minute.

5. Add tomatoes and cook till soft.

6. Add marinated chicken, fenugreek leaves and mix well. Cover and simmer till chicken is almost done. Adjust seasoning.

7. Sprinkle *kasoori methi*, ginger strips and coriander leaves. Remove from heat and keep covered for five minutes before serving.

Non-Veg | Preparation 30 mins | Cooking 20 mins | Serves 4 people

Sweet *and Sour* Chicken

INGREDIENTS

400 grams boneless chicken, cut into 1 inch pieces

3 tablespoons cornflour

4 tablespoons tomato sauce

2 tablespoons sugar

½ cup pineapple juice

¼ teaspoon MSG (optional)

½ teaspoon white pepper powder

Salt to taste

3 cups Chicken Stock (pg. 120)

1 inch ginger, finely chopped

4-6 garlic cloves, finely chopped

1 medium onion, quartered and layers separated

1 medium green capsicum, seeded

½ medium red capsicum, seeded

½ medium yellow capsicum, seeded

1 pineapple slice

2 tablespoons vinegar

1 Apply salt to the chicken pieces and set aside for fifteen minutes.

2 Mixed cornflour and one cup of chicken stock.

3 Mix tomato sauce, sugar, pineapple juice, MSG, white pepper powder and salt with one cup of chicken stock.

4 Cut the green, red and yellow capsicums and pineapple into one inch pieces.

5 Heat a non-stick pan, add ginger and garlic and cook for one minute.

6 Add onion and continue to cook for a minute more.

7 Stir in sauce and spice mix, green, red and yellow capsicums, remaining stock and chicken pieces. Cook for four to five minutes. Add the cornflour mixture and cook till the sauce starts to thicken, stirring continuously.

8 Add pineapple pieces and vinegar. Mix and take off the heat. Serve hot.

Non-Veg | Preparation 20 mins | Cooking 10 mins | Serves 4 people

Chicken *Stew*

INGREDIENTS

800 grams chicken on the bone, cut into 1½ inch pieces

7-8 garlic cloves, sliced

2 medium onions, sliced

2 medium carrots, cut into 1 inch cubes

2 medium potatoes, cut into 1 inch cubes

2 tablespoons wholewheat flour (*atta*)

Salt to taste

5 cups Chicken Stock (pg. 120)

¼ teaspoon black pepper powder

6-8 French beans, cut into 1 inch pieces

½ cup skimmed milk

1 Heat a non-stick pan and add garlic, onions, carrots and potatoes and roast for four to five minutes on high heat.

2 Add wholewheat flour to the vegetables and roast for a minute. Add chicken pieces and salt and cook for three to four minutes. Add stock and bring to a boil. Add half the pepper powder. Cover and cook for three to four minutes.

3 Uncover, add French beans, mix and cook for a minute. Add the milk and the remaining pepper powder. Cover and cook on medium heat for seven to eight minutes.

4 Serve hot.

Non-Veg | Preparation 10 mins | Cooking 20 mins | Serves 4 people

Chicken

Stew

Spicy Salsa Chicken

INGREDIENTS

2 boneless chicken breasts, (200 grams each), cut into 1-inch pieces

FOR THE SALSA

Concassé of 5 medium tomatoes (pg. 78)

1 medium onion, chopped

4 garlic cloves, chopped

2-3 jalapeno chillies, chopped

½ teaspoon oregano

Salt to taste

7-8 black peppercorns, crushed

1 tablespoon lemon juice

1 teaspoon fresh parsley, chopped

6 olives, stoned and chopped

2 tablespoons fresh coriander leaves, chopped

1 lemon, sliced

1 Mix tomato concassé, onion, garlic, jalapenos, oregano, salt, peppercorns, lemon juice, parsley and olives together.

2 Marinate chicken cubes in this mixture for about fifteen minutes.

3 Heat a deep non-stick pan and cook the marinated chicken cubes till done, stirring occasionally.

4 Serve hot garnished with coriander leaves and lemon slices.

Non-Veg | Preparation 15 mins | Cooking 15 mins | Serves 4 people

Lemon Chicken

INGREDIENTS

4 boneless chicken breasts, (200 grams each), cut into 1 inch pieces

3 tablespoons lemon juice

Salt to taste

2 tablespoons cornflour

1 small green capsicum, seeded

½ small red capsicum, seeded

½ small yellow capsicum, seeded

2½ cups Chicken Stock (pg. 120)

½ teaspoon white pepper powder

¼ teaspoon MSG (optional)

3 tablespoons sugar

1 star anise (*chakri phool/badiyan*)

1 teaspoon lemon rind, grated

1 Marinate chicken in one tablespoon of lemon juice and salt for half an hour. Mix cornflour with half a cup of chicken stock. Cut the green, red and yellow capsicums into one inch pieces.

2 Heat a non-stick pan. Add green, red and yellow capsicums, chicken and remaining chicken stock and bring to a boil.

3 Add white pepper powder, MSG, sugar, star anise and lemon rind and cook till chicken is done. Add cornflour mixture and cook for a minute or till the sauce thickens. Stir in the remaining lemon juice and serve hot.

Non-Veg | Preparation 30 mins | Cooking 15 mins | Serves 4 people

Baked Mince

INGREDIENTS

2 cups chicken mince (400 grams)

5-6 garlic cloves, chopped

2 medium onions, chopped

1 medium carrot, chopped

1 celery stalk, chopped

½ cup Chicken Stock (pg. 120)

1½ teaspoons Worcestershire sauce

Salt to taste

7-8 black peppercorns, crushed

½ cup tomato purée

2-3 sprigs fresh parsley

¼ teaspoon black pepper powder

A pinch of nutmeg powder

9 tablespoons skimmed milk

4-5 medium potatoes, boiled and mashed

1. In a non-stick frying pan roast chicken mince, garlic and onion on low heat for two to three minutes. Add carrot and celery. Stir and add chicken stock. Cover and simmer till the mince is cooked.

2. Stir in Worcestershire sauce, salt, crushed peppercorns and tomato purée and cook for another minute.

3. Preheat the oven to 200°C/400°F/Gas Mark 6. Chop parsley reserving one sprig for garnishing.

4. Add salt, black pepper powder, chopped parsley, nutmeg powder and milk to mashed potatoes and mix well. Put the mixture into a piping bag with a star nozzle.

5. Spread the prepared mince in a glass baking dish. Pipe the mashed potatoes on top in rosettes.

6. Bake in the oven for ten to twelve minutes or till the potatoes turn golden.

7. Serve hot garnished with the reserved sprig of parsley.

Non-Veg | Preparation 15 mins | Cooking 30 mins | Serves 4 people

Saag Gosht

INGREDIENTS

3 medium bunches (350 grams each) spinach

600 grams boneless lamb/mutton, cut into 1½ inch cubes

¾ cup skimmed milk yogurt

1 tablespoon ginger-garlic paste

½ teaspoon turmeric powder

2 teaspoons red chilli powder

½ teaspoon coriander powder

1 teaspoon *garam masala* powder

Salt to taste

3-4 green chillies

2 bay leaves

3 green cardamoms

1 black cardamom

6 cloves

1 inch cinnamon

6-8 black peppercorns

1 teaspoon cumin seeds

6-8 garlic cloves, chopped

3 medium onions, sliced

1 inch ginger, cut into thin strips

½ tablespoon dill leaves (*suva*), chopped

1 teaspoon dried fenugreek leaves (*kasoori methi*), roasted and crushed

1 Mix together half a cup of yogurt, ginger-garlic paste, turmeric powder, one teaspoon of red chilli powder, the coriander powder, *garam masala* powder and salt to taste. Marinate the lamb cubes in this mixture for about half an hour.

2 Blanch spinach in boiling salted water for one minute. Drain and refresh in cold water. Grind spinach and green chillies together to a coarse paste. Set aside.

3 Heat a thick-bottomed pan. Add bay leaves, green cardamoms, black cardamom, cloves, cinnamon, peppercorns, cumin seeds and roast till they emit a fragrant aroma. Add garlic and roast till it turns light brown. Add onions and cook till translucent.

4 Add half the ginger strips, remaining red chilli powder and marinated lamb cubes. Cook on high heat, stirring continuously for two minutes. Add remaining yogurt and one cup of water and bring to a boil. Transfer the mixture into a pressure cooker and cook till the cooker gives out eight whistles.

5 Wait till the pressure reduces. Open the lid, add spinach paste, dill leaves and salt if necessary. Cook till lamb is tender and well-coated with spinach.

6 Sprinkle *kasoori methi* and serve hot, garnished with remaining ginger strips.

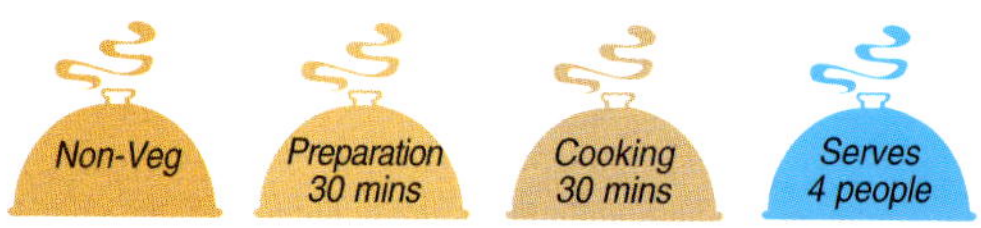

INGREDIENTS

250 grams penne

5 medium tomatoes

6 garlic cloves, crushed

2 medium onions, sliced

1 teaspoon crushed red chillies

1 tablespoon oregano

Salt to taste

5-6 basil leaves

Penne Arrabbiata

1 Blanch tomatoes, peel, remove seeds and coarsely chop.

2 Cook penne in plenty of salted boiling water, drain, refresh in cold water and set aside.

3 Heat a non-stick pan, add garlic and roast until light brown.

4 Add onions, roast until transluscent and then add crushed red chillies, oregano and tomatoes.

5 Cook for about five minutes on low heat. Add salt and mix well.

6 Add penne and roughly torn basil leaves and toss lightly. Serve hot.

INGREDIENTS

1½ cups brown rice

2 medium carrots, cut into ½ inch cubes

10-12 French beans, cut into ½ inch pieces

¼ medium cauliflower, separated into small florets

6-7 medium fresh button mushrooms, (optional) halved

½ cup green peas, shelled

1 bay leaf

2-3 cloves

1 teaspoon cumin seeds

1 inch cinnamon

2 green chillies, slit

Salt to taste

2 tablespoons fresh coriander leaves, finely chopped

Brown Rice

Vegetable Pilaf

1 Soak brown rice in four to five cups of water for two hours. Drain and set aside.

2 Heat a deep non-stick pan, add bay leaf, cloves, cumin seeds and cinnamon and roast for a few seconds or till fragrant. Add drained rice and roast for one to two minutes more. Add four cups of water and bring to a boil.

3 Add carrots, French beans, cauliflower, mushrooms and green chillies. Stir and bring to a boil. Add salt and mix. Lower heat, cover and cook till almost done.

4 Add green peas and mix gently. Cover and cook till done.

5 Serve hot, garnished with fresh coriander leaves.

Note: *Brown rice is available at health food stores.*

Veg | Preparation 2 hrs | Cooking 25 mins | Serves 4 people

Penne
Arrabbiata
Brown Rice
Vegetable
Pilaf

Chicken Kofta Pulao

INGREDIENTS

250 grams chicken mince

1½ cups Basmati rice

4-5 green cardamoms

1 bay leaf

7-8 cloves

Salt to taste

4 tablespoons fresh coriander leaves, finely chopped

1 inch ginger, finely chopped

1½ teaspoons red chilli powder

20 black peppercorns, crushed

½ teaspoon green cardamom powder

2 medium onions, finely chopped

3 medium tomatoes, finely chopped

1 teaspoon coriander powder

½ teaspoon cumin powder

½ teaspoon *garam masala* powder

1 Soak rice in four to five cups of water for fifteen to twenty minutes. Drain and set aside.

2 Boil six cups of water in a deep pan with green cardamoms, bay leaf, cloves and salt for about five minutes. Strain and set aside.

3 Take chicken mince in a bowl and add two tablespoons of coriander leaves, ginger, half the red chilli powder and crushed peppercorns, and the green cardamom powder. Add salt to taste. Mix well and make marble-sized *koftas*.

4 Boil the *koftas* in the flavoured water till cooked. Drain and set aside. Reserve the cooking liquid.

5 Heat a deep non-stick pan and roast onions till translucent. Add chopped tomatoes, remaining red chilli powder and crushed peppercorns, coriander powder and cumin powder. Add salt and sauté till tomatoes are cooked.

6 Add drained rice and cook for two to three minutes. Add three cups of reserved cooking liquid and one cup of water. Bring to a boil, cover tightly with a lid and simmer for ten minutes.

7 Uncover the pan, add the cooked chicken *koftas* and mix gently. Cover and cook for two to three minutes. Sprinkle *garam masala* powder and the remaining coriander leaves. Serve hot with a *raita* of your choice.

Non-Veg | Preparation 20 mins | Cooking 30 mins | Serves 4 people

INGREDIENTS

250 grams wholewheat spaghetti

1 medium carrot, cut into 1 inch cubes

1 small head broccoli, separated into small florets

8-10 fresh button mushrooms, halved

1 medium green capsicum, cut into 1 inch pieces

3 tablespoons wholewheat flour (*atta*)

1½ cups skimmed milk

½ teaspoon mixed herbs, roasted

Salt to taste

¼ teaspoon white pepper powder

1 tablespoon fresh parsley, chopped

Spaghetti with Mixed Vegetables

and Herb Sauce

1 Boil the spaghetti in five cups of water till just done. Drain, refresh in cold water and set aside.

2 Blanch carrot and broccoli separately in one cup of boiling water for two to three minutes. Drain and refresh in cold water.

3 For the herb sauce, lightly roast wholewheat flour in a non-stick pan. Add milk and whisk rapidly so that no lumps form. Strain if required. Add salt, pepper and mixed herbs. Mix and set aside.

4 In a non-stick pan add the carrots, broccoli, mushrooms, capsicum and spaghetti, toss well and cook on moderate heat for two minutes.

5 Add the herb sauce and mix well. Adjust seasonings.

6 Serve garnished with chopped parsley.

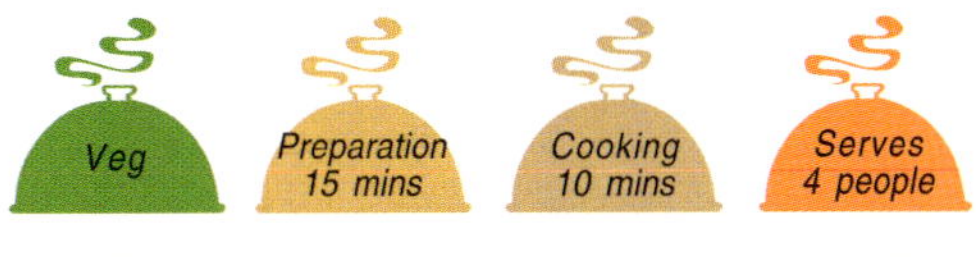

Chholay

Biryani

Chholay

Biryani

INGREDIENTS

1½ cups Basmati rice
1 cup chickpeas (*Kabuli chana*)
2 tablespoons tea leaves
Salt to taste
5-6 green cardamoms
2-3 bay leaves
2-3 cloves
1½ cups skimmed milk yogurt
1 teaspoon ginger paste
1 inch ginger, cut into thin strips
½ cup fresh mint leaves
1 teaspoon green chilli paste
1 teaspoon red chilli powder
1 teaspoon turmeric powder
1 teaspoon *garam masala* powder
1 teaspoon garlic paste
A few strands of saffron
1 tablespoon skimmed milk
A few drops of *kewra* water
¼ cup fresh coriander leaves, chopped

1 Soak *Kabuli chana* overnight or for six hours in four cups of water. Drain and pressure cook in four cups of fresh water with salt and tea leaves tied in a piece of muslin, till tender. Remove the muslin bag and drain chickpeas.

2 Marinate boiled chickpeas in yogurt, ginger paste, ginger strips, half the mint leaves, green chilli paste, red chilli powder, turmeric powder, *garam masala* powder and garlic paste.

3 Soak rice in three cups of water for about half an hour. Drain. Boil four cups of water in a deep pan with salt, green cardamoms, bay leaves and cloves. Add rice and cook till half done. Drain.

4 Dissolve saffron in warm milk and mix in *kewra* water. Place the marinated chickpeas in a deep non-stick pan.

5 Spread cooked rice over the chickpeas evenly. Sprinkle dissolved saffron and half the coriander leaves over the rice.

6 Cover the pan tightly and cook on low heat for fifteen minutes or till rice is done. Serve hot, garnished with remaining coriander and mint leaves.

Chef's Tip: *You can use chholay masala to add more flavour to this biryani.*

Veg | Preparation 90 mins | Cooking 30 mins | Serves 4 people

INGREDIENTS

1½ cups Basmati rice

1 medium carrot, cut into ½ inch diamonds

10 French beans, ½ inch diamonds

¼ small cauliflower, separated into florets

2 medium tomatoes, chopped

1 bay leaf

½ teaspoon cumin seeds

2 inches cinnamon

2 black cardamoms

1 inch ginger, chopped

7-8 Madras *(sambhar)* onions, peeled and halved

Salt to taste

7-8 black peppercorns, crushed

½ teaspoon red chilli powder

½ teaspoon *garam masala* powder

1 tablespoon lemon juice

3 tablespoons fresh coriander leaves, chopped

Mixed Vegetables *and Tomato* Pulao

1 Soak rice in three cups of water for half an hour. Drain and set aside.

2 Heat a deep non-stick pan and dry roast bay leaf, cumin seeds, cinnamon and black cardamoms till fragrant. Add ginger, Madras onions, tomatoes and salt to taste. Stir and cook for two to three minutes.

3 Add three cups of water and stir. Bring to a boil and add carrot, French beans, cauliflower, rice, crushed peppercorns, red chilli powder and *garam masala* powder and stir gently, but continuously for three to four minutes.

4 Adjust salt. Cover and cook on low heat till done. Add lemon juice and mix.

5 Serve hot, garnished with coriander leaves.

Veg | Preparation 30 mins | Cooking 15 mins | Serves 4 people

Palak Raita

INGREDIENTS

2 medium bunches (350 grams each) spinach

1 green chilli

2 cups skimmed milk yogurt

Black salt to taste

1 teaspoon roasted cumin powder

Salt to taste

1 Blanch one bunch of spinach in boiling water, drain and refresh in cold water. Drain, squeeze out excess water and purée with one green chilli in a blender. Shred the remaining spinach.

2 Whisk yogurt and add spinach purée, black salt and roasted cumin powder. Mix well and chill in the refrigerator.

3 Heat a non-stick pan. Add shredded spinach and cook over high heat for three to four minutes, stirring continuously.

4 Season with salt and mix well. Continue to cook on high heat till the spinach is almost dry. Take the pan off the heat and cool.

5 Mix the spinach with the flavoured yogurt just before serving. Adjust salt and serve chilled.

Veg | Preparation 10 mins | Cooking 10 mins | Serves 4 people

Masaledar Dal

INGREDIENTS

½ cup split pigeon peas (*toovar/arhar dal*)

Salt to taste

¼ teaspoon turmeric powder

2-3 green chillies, slit

1 teaspoon cumin seeds

3-4 whole dried red chillies

A pinch of asafoetida

2 medium onions, chopped

½ teaspoon red chilli powder

1 teaspoon coriander powder

2 medium tomatoes, chopped

½ teaspoon *garam masala* powder

2 teaspoons lemon juice

2 tablespoons fresh coriander leaves, chopped

1. Soak *dal* in four cups of water for half an hour. Drain and pressure cook with two cups of water, salt, turmeric powder and green chillies till done.
2. Heat a deep non-stick pan. Roast cumin seeds, whole red chillies, asafoetida and onions for two to three minutes.
3. Add red chilli powder, coriander powder and tomatoes and cook for a further five minutes on moderate heat.
4. Add cooked *dal* and mix well. Add *garam masala* powder, more salt if necessary and simmer for five to ten minutes.
5. Add lemon juice and coriander leaves and stir to mix.
6. Serve hot with steamed rice.

Veg | Preparation 30 mins | Cooking 30 mins | Serves 4 people

Tamatar *ki Kadhi*

INGREDIENTS

12 small tomatoes, puréed

4 teaspoons gram flour (*besan*)

½ teaspoon turmeric powder

1 teaspoon red chilli powder

Salt to taste

1 teaspoon sugar

½ teaspoon mustard seeds

A pinch of asafoetida

½ teaspoon cumin seeds

5-6 curry leaves

4-5 whole red chillies

2 tablespoons fresh coriander leaves, chopped

1. Mix tomato purée, gram flour, turmeric powder, red chilli powder, salt and sugar. Whisk till well blended. Stir in two cups of water.
2. Heat a deep non-stick pan and roast mustard seeds, asafoetida, cumin seeds, curry leaves and whole red chillies till fragrant.
3. Add the tomato mixture and bring to a boil. Reduce heat and simmer for ten minutes.
4. Serve hot, garnished with coriander leaves.

Veg | Preparation 15 mins | Cooking 15 mins | Serves 4 people

Beetroot *Raita*

INGREDIENTS

1 small beetroot

2 cups skimmed milk yogurt, whisked

1 teaspoon roasted cumin powder

½ teaspoon red chilli powder

1 tablespoon fresh coriander leaves, finely chopped

Salt to taste

1. Boil, peel and grate beetroot. Chill in the refrigerator.
2. Add roasted cumin powder, red chilli powder, fresh coriander leaves and salt to yogurt and mix well.
3. Add chilled beetroot and mix gently.
4. Serve chilled.

Veg | Preparation 30 mins | Cooking 5 mins | Serves 4 people

Lauki Chana *Dal*

Tamatar *ki Kadh*

Beetroot *Raita*

Lauki Chana Dal

INGREDIENTS

½ cup split Bengal gram (*chana dal*)

½ small bottle gourd (*lauki*), peeled, cut into 1 inch cubes

Salt to taste

½ teaspoon turmeric powder

½ teaspoon cumin seeds

2 green chillies, chopped

A pinch of asafoetida

½ teaspoon red chilli powder

2 teaspoons coriander powder

2 medium tomatoes, chopped

½ teaspoon *garam masala* powder

¼ teaspoon sugar

2 teaspoons lemon juice

2 tablespoons fresh coriander leaves, chopped

1 Soak *chana dal* in one and half cups of water for an hour. Drain.

2 Boil *chana dal* and *lauki* with salt, turmeric powder and three cups of water till done. Mash lightly with the back of a rounded spoon and mix well. Set aside.

3 Heat a non-stick pan. Add cumin seeds, green chillies and asafoetida and cook for a minute. Add red chilli powder, coriander powder and two tablespoons of water and cook till fragrant.

4 Add tomatoes and cook till they soften.

5 Add cooked *chana dal* and *lauki* and stir to mix. Add *garam masala* powder, sugar and more salt if necessary. Simmer for two minutes.

6 Add lemon juice and stir. Garnish with coriander leaves and serve hot.

Veg | Preparation 1 hr | Cooking 25 mins | Serves 4 people

INGREDIENTS

1 medium red capsicum, seeded and quartered

5 medium tomatoes, seeded and quartered

5-6 garlic cloves , chopped fine

Salt to taste

2 teaspoons sugar

2 tablespoons lemon juice

1 sprig fresh parsley

Roasted *Capsicum* and Tomato *Dip*

1 Preheat oven to 180°C/350°F/Gas Mark 4.

2 Arrange red capsicum and tomato together with garlic on a baking tray. Sprinkle with salt.

3 Bake for twenty to twenty-five minutes and allow to cool. When cool, peel capsicum and tomato wedges and chop.

4 Heat a non-stick pan and roast garlic for a minute. Add capsicum and tomatoes and cook for two minutes. Add more salt, if necessary and the sugar. Mix well.

5 Cook for another two minutes and add lemon juice. Mix again. Serve garnished with a sprig of parsley.

Note: *When in a hurry, purée baked capsicums, tomatoes and garlic without peeling and cook till done.*

Veg | Preparation 10 mins | Cooking 35 mins | Serves 4 people

Palak and Chhenna Parantha

INGREDIENTS

2 cups wholewheat flour (*atta*) + extra for dusting

1 medium bunch spinach, (350 grams) chopped

100 grams skimmed milk cottage cheese (*chhenna/paneer*)

½ cup skimmed milk yogurt, whisked + to serve

1 small onion, finely chopped

½ teaspoon carom seeds (*ajwain*)

2 tablespoons fresh coriander leaves, chopped

2 tablespoons fresh mint leaves

2 green chillies, chopped

½ teaspoon cumin powder

1 teaspoon *chaat masala*

1 teaspoon *garam masala* powder

Salt to taste

1. Take wholewheat flour in a deep bowl.
2. Add remaining ingredients and knead into a medium soft dough with sufficient water. Cover and rest the dough for fifteen minutes.
3. Divide the dough into twelve equal portions and shape into balls.
4. Roll out into thick *paranthas*. Heat a *tawa* and roast *paranthas* on moderate heat on both sides till brown and crisp.
5. Serve hot with skimmed milk yogurt.

Veg | Preparation 15 mins | Cooking 20 mins | Serves 4 people

INGREDIENTS

2 cups wholewheat flour (*atta*)

¼ cup fresh coriander leaves, chopped

¼ cup fresh mint leaves, chopped

Salt to taste

2 teaspoons *chaat masala*

½ cup skimmed milk yogurt

Dhania *Pudina* Parantha

1 Place the wholewheat flour and salt in a bowl. Add coriander leaves, mint leaves and enough water to make a soft dough. Cover and rest the dough for twenty to twenty-five minutes.

2 Divide the dough into eight equal portions and shape into balls.

3 Mix yogurt and *chaat masala*.

4 Roll out each ball into a medium-sized *chapati*. Spread with a tablespoon of the yogurt mixture. Fold the *chapati* like a fan and twist it back into the form of a ball. Set aside for five minutes.

5 Roll out each portion into a *parantha* of five to seven inches diameter. Cook on a hot non-stick *tawa* till both sides are a light golden brown.

6 Before serving, crush the *paranthas* lightly between your palms to open out the layers.

Veg | Preparation 25 mins | Cooking 25 mins | Serves 4 people

Green Mango and Onion
Chutney

Dhania Pudina
Parantha

Date and Tamarind Chutney

INGREDIENTS

15-20 dates (*khajur*)

1 cup tamarind pulp

2 teaspoons cumin seeds

¼ teaspoon fennel seeds (*saunf*)

½ cup jaggery, grated

2 teaspoons red chilli powder

1 teaspoon dried ginger powder (*soonth*)

1 teaspoon black salt

Salt to taste

1 Wash dates, stone and chop roughly. Dry roast cumin seeds and fennel seeds. Cool slightly and grind to a powder. Mix together dates, tamarind pulp, cumin and fennel powder, jaggery, red chilli powder, dried ginger powder, black salt, salt and four cups of water.

2 Cook on moderate heat till the mixture comes to a boil, lower heat and simmer for six to eight minutes, or till the chutney is thick. Cool and serve, or store for later use.

Veg | Preparation 10 mins | Cooking 10 mins | Serves 4 people

Green Mango and Onion Chutney

INGREDIENTS

3 medium green, unripe mangoes, peeled, stoned and chopped

2 medium onions, grated

4-6 green chillies, chopped

1 tablespoon pomegranate seeds (*anardana*)

2 tablespoons lemon juice

½ teaspoon black salt

Salt to taste

½ teaspoon sugar

1 Put the green mangoes, green chillies, pomegranate seeds, lemon juice, salt and sugar into a blender and blend till smooth.

2 Adjust the consistency by adding water. Squeeze the grated onion to remove excess juice and add to the chutney.

Veg | Preparation 10 mins | Cooking nil | Serves 4 people

Pineapple *Yogurt Fool*

INGREDIENTS

½ medium fresh pineapple, cut into small cubes

½ cup sugar

1 inch cinnamon

½ cup drained skimmed milk yogurt

1 Mix pineapple, sugar and cinnamon in a pan and stew for thirty minutes. Set aside to cool.

2 Remove pineapple pieces and mix with drained yogurt. Process together in a blender. Chill in the refrigerator. Serve chilled.

Veg | Preparation 10 mins | Cooking 40 mins | Serves 4 people

Sitaphal *Basoondi*

INGREDIENTS

1½ litres (7½ cups) skimmed milk

1 cup sitaphal (custard apple) pulp

½ cup sugar

½ teaspoon green cardamom powder

10-12 pistachios, sliced

1 tablespoon *charoli* (*chironjee*)

10-12 almonds, blanched and slivered

3-4 rose petals (optional)

1 Bring the milk to a boil in a heavy bottomed pan on high heat. Lower heat and simmer for half an hour. Keep stirring so that the milk does not burn and stick to the bottom of the pan. When the milk reduces to half the original quantity, add sugar. Simmer for five more minutes. Take the pan off the heat and set aside to cool.

2 When cool, add custard apple, green cardamom powder, sliced pistachios and *charoli*. Transfer to a serving bowl and garnish with almond slivers and rose petals. Serve cold.

Veg | Preparation 10 mins | Cooking 30 mins | Serves 4 people

Zafrani

Sevian

INGREDIENTS

6 tablespoons vermicelli (*sevian*)

10-15 saffron strands

1½ litres (7½ cups) skimmed milk

8 tablespoons sugar

20 raisins (*kishmish*)

1 teaspoon green cardamom powder

1 tablespoon almond slivers, toasted

1 Heat a non-stick pan and roast vermicelli on moderate heat till lightly browned.

2 Pour milk into a deep pan and bring to a boil. Lower heat and simmer till reduced to half the quantity.

3 Add sugar and cook till it dissolves. Add vermicelli and raisins and cook for two minutes.

4 Take the pan off the heat. Add saffron and green cardamom powder and stir well.

5 Serve hot or cold, decorated with toasted almond slivers.

Veg | Preparation 10 mins | Cooking 45 mins | Serves 4 people

Zafrani Sevian

Suji Kheer

INGREDIENTS

½ cup semolina (*suji/rawa*)

1½ litres (7½ cups) skimmed milk

7-8 strands saffron

½ cup sugar

2 tablespoons *charoli* (*chironjee*)

20 almonds, blanched and slivered

1 Roast *suji* in a thick-bottomed pan on low heat for fifteen minutes or till light brown.

2 Soak saffron in one tablespoon of milk.

3 Bring remaining milk to a boil and simmer on moderate heat till reduced to one litre.

4 Add thickened milk to *suji*, stirring continuously to prevent lumps from forming.

5 Cook on high heat till it comes to a boil. Add sugar and simmer for two to three minutes.

6 Add saffron and stir well.

7 Decorate with *charoli* and almond slivers and serve hot or cold.

Veg | Preparation 15 mins | Cooking 25 mins | Serves 4 people

Chhannar *Payesh*

INGREDIENTS

- ½ cup *chhenna (paneer)*, made from skimmed cow's milk
- 1 litre (5 cups) skimmed milk
- ½ cup sugar
- 5-6 almonds, blanched and chopped
- 7-8 pistachios, blanched and chopped

1. Boil milk, lower heat and simmer till reduced to half the original quantity. Add sugar and cook till it dissolves.
2. Mash *chhenna* in a bowl. Add it to the milk. Simmer for two minutes. Sprinkle chopped nuts and serve cold.

Chef's Tip: *If cow's milk chhenna is not available use chhenna made from buffalo's milk. I recommend chhenna made from cow's milk because it is low in fat.*

Veg | *Preparation 15 mins* | *Cooking 30 mins* | *Serves 4 people*

Gajar *ki Kheer*

INGREDIENTS

- 2 medium carrots, grated
- 1 litre (5 cups) skimmed milk
- $^{1}/_{3}$ cup sugar
- ¼ teaspoon green cardamom powder
- 2 tablespoons raisins (*kishmish*)

1. Bring the milk to a boil, reduce heat and simmer till it is reduced to three-fourth its original volume.
2. Add carrots and cook on low heat for about fifteen to twenty minutes or till the carrots are completely cooked. Add sugar and cook, stirring occasionally, till sugar dissolves.
3. Add green cardamom powder and stir well. Serve garnished with raisins.

Veg | *Preparation 10 mins* | *Cooking 30 mins* | *Serves 4 people*

Anjeer

ka Meetha

Sitapha

Basoond

INGREDIENTS

250 grams dried figs (*anjeer*)

250 grams dried, seedless dates

¼ cup skimmed milk powder

4-5 almonds, roasted and slivered

Anjeer *ka Meetha*

1. Soak figs in three cups of water for three to four hours. Boil them in the same water in which they were soaked, for three to five minutes.

2. Take the pan off the heat, drain the figs and cool slightly. Reserve some figs and purée the rest. Chop the reserved figs.

3. Chop dates roughly and soak in two cups of hot water for fifteen to twenty minutes. Drain and purée.

4. Mix the two purées and add skimmed milk powder. Mix well and cook on low heat for fifteen to twenty minutes or till well blended.

5. Add the chopped figs and simmer for another two to three minutes.

6. Serve garnished with almond slivers.

Veg | Preparation 3 hrs | Cooking 25 mins | Serves 4 people

Annexure

Chicken Stock

Boil 200 grams chicken bones in water for 5 minutes. Drain and discard water. Boil blanched bones with a roughly chopped carrot, celery stalk, leek, 2-3 parsley stalks, 6-7 black peppercorns, 5-6 cloves, 1 bay leaf and 10 cups of water. Remove any scum which rises to the surface and replace it with more cold water. Simmer for at least 1 hour. Remove from heat, strain, cool and store in a refrigerator till further use.

Goda Masala Powder

Roast 1 cup coriander seeds, 2 tablespoons cumin seeds, ¼ cup stone flower, 6 two-inch sticks cinnamon, 16 green cardamoms, 25 cloves, ¾ teaspoon caraway seeds, 10-12 black peppercorns, 10-12 bay leaves, 1 teaspoon *nagkeshar,* 2 blades mace, 3 tablespoons dried coconut, grated, 1 teaspoon sesame seeds, 3 whole red chillies and 1 teaspoon asafoetida separately one by one. Cool and grind to a fine powder. Bottle. Makes 100 grams of *goda masala* powder.

Vegetable Stock

Peel, wash and chop 1 onion, ½ medium carrot, 2-3 inch stalk celery and 2-3 garlic cloves. Place in a pan with 1 bay leaf, 5-6 peppercorns, 2-3 cloves and five cups of water and bring to a boil. Lower heat and simmer for fifteen minutes and strain. Cool and store in a refrigerator till further use.

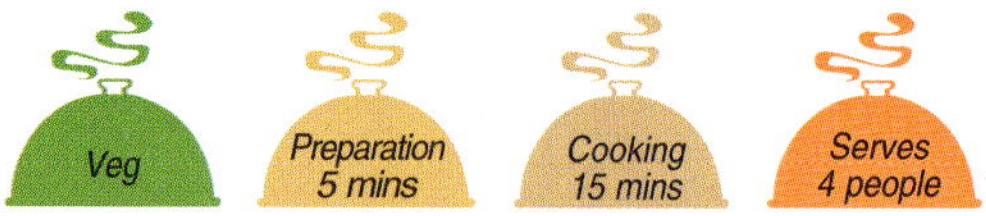